# Quantum Physics and Higher Consciousness

*Unlocking the Mysteries of Reality and Awakening Your Inner Power*

© Copyright 2025 - All rights reserved.

The content contained within this book may not be reproduced, duplicated, or transmitted without direct written permission from the author or the publisher.

Under no circumstances will any blame or legal responsibility be held against the publisher or author for any damages, reparation, or monetary loss due to the information contained within this book, either directly or indirectly.

**Legal Notice:**

This book is copyright-protected. It is only for personal use. You cannot amend, distribute, sell, use, quote, or paraphrase any part of the content within this book without the consent of the author or publisher.

**Disclaimer Notice:**

Please note the information contained within this document is for educational and entertainment purposes only. All effort has been executed to present accurate, up-to-date, reliable, and complete information. No warranties of any kind are declared or implied. Readers acknowledge that the author is not engaging in the rendering of legal, financial, medical, or professional advice. The content within this book has been derived from various sources. Please consult a licensed professional before attempting any techniques outlined in this book.

By reading this document, the reader agrees that under no circumstances is the author responsible for any losses, direct or indirect, that are incurred as a result of the use of the information contained within this document, including, but not limited to, errors, omissions, or inaccuracies.

# Your Free Gift
# (only available for a limited time)

Thanks for getting this book! If you want to learn more about various spirituality topics, then join Mari Silva's community and get a free guided meditation MP3 for awakening your third eye. This guided meditation mp3 is designed to open and strengthen ones third eye so you can experience a higher state of consciousness. Simply visit the link below the image to get started.

https://spiritualityspot.com/meditation

Or, Scan the QR code!

# Table of Contents

PART 1: QUANTUM PHYSICS FOR BEGINNERS .................................................. 1
    INTRODUCTION .................................................................................................... 2
    CHAPTER 1: INTRODUCTION TO QUANTUM PHYSICS ........................... 4
    CHAPTER 2: EXPLORING PARTICLE BEHAVIOR ..................................... 15
    CHAPTER 3: WHAT IS LIGHT? ........................................................................ 24
    CHAPTER 4: QUANTUM OBSERVATIONS, EXPERIMENTS, AND THEIR INTERPRETATIONS ................................................................... 35
    CHAPTER 5: QUANTUM REALITY AND CONSCIOUSNESS ................... 47
    CHAPTER 6: QUANTUM MYSTICISM – SCIENCE AND SPIRITUALITY ................................................................................................... 60
    CHAPTER 7: ENTANGLEMENT – EVERYTHING IS CONNECTED ..................................................................................................... 71
    CHAPTER 8: SUPERPOSITION: ANYTHING IS POSSIBLE ...................... 81
    CHAPTER 9: THE MULTIVERSE .................................................................... 90
    CONCLUSION ...................................................................................................... 99
PART 2: HIGHER CONSCIOUSNESS ............................................................... 101
    INTRODUCTION ............................................................................................... 102
    CHAPTER 1: WHAT IS HIGHER CONSCIOUSNESS? ............................... 104
    CHAPTER 2: THE QUANTUM COSMOS .................................................... 118
    CHAPTER 3: TAP INTO YOUR INNER POWER ........................................ 130
    CHAPTER 4: GO BEYOND TO EXPAND YOUR AWARENESS ............... 140
    CHAPTER 5: MEET YOUR HIGHER SELF .................................................. 151
    CHAPTER 6: WORK WITH SPIRIT GUIDES .............................................. 158

CHAPTER 7: TIMELINES, PAST LIVES, AND SOUL CONTRACTS .................................................................. 166
CHAPTER 8: YOUR HIGHER PURPOSE REVEALED ............................... 175
CHAPTER 9: DAILY RITUALS FOR CONSCIOUS LIVING ....................... 187
CONCLUSION ........................................................................................ 195
HERE'S ANOTHER BOOK BY MARI SILVA THAT YOU MIGHT LIKE .................................................................................................... 198
YOUR FREE GIFT (ONLY AVAILABLE FOR A LIMITED TIME) ................. 199
REFERENCES ........................................................................................ 200
IMAGE SOURCES ................................................................................. 204

# Part 1: Quantum Physics for Beginners

*Unraveling the Fundamentals of Quantum Mechanics, Particle Behavior, and the Nature of Reality along with the Interplay between Science and Spirituality*

# Introduction

If you know next to nothing about physics, let alone quantum physics, this topic may initially appear intimidating. However, with this book in your hands, you won't feel that way for much longer. If you've always wanted to know what the secrets of the subatomic world are, and you want to dig up the mysteries shrouded in scientific jargon, you couldn't have picked a better book for the job than this. No scientific background? No problem. Every complex concept of quantum physics is broken down into language that is easy to understand. You won't have to grapple with complex formulas or try to work out complex equations, either.

Unlike other books on the topic of quantum physics, this book is suitable for beginners. The concepts are clear and explained in engaging language. It is a book full of carefully deconstructed concepts to help you understand the incredibly quirky world of quantum physics.

It offers so much more to readers than just an understanding of this branch of science. This book is excellent for those who've always sought the bridge between spirituality and science. It is full of practical information demonstrating how to improve your life. By the final page, you'll discover that your understanding of reality is deeper and richer than it has ever been.

It is no accident you've chosen this book from all the others you could be reading right now. You've been handed a passport to the power to unlock every world you could think of. If you boldly choose to continue reading, rest assured that your life will no longer remain the same. Therefore, you should exercise caution and only dive into this book if you are prepared to have your socks knocked off.

You will learn everything you need to know about reality, consciousness, and your specific purpose in life. This is no ordinary textbook. This is a whole experience, one you're not about to forget. So, if you are prepared for the new, the strange, and the extraordinary, there's not a moment left to lose. Begin with the first chapter and discover the magic in reality.

# Chapter 1: Introduction to Quantum Physics

Suppose you know nothing about the sciences like physics. In that case, quantum physics may seem like such an intimidating topic that you'd never normally touch it with a ten-foot pole. As you'll soon discover, it's not that difficult to understand. This chapter will introduce you to quantum physics, keeping things as beginner-friendly as possible. You don't have to worry about pulling your hair out to understand the concepts. That's a guarantee.

Welcome to Quantum Physics. An electron around a nucleus.[1]

# The Puzzle of Quantum Physics

Hello, Alice. Sure, that's not your actual name, but it might as well be because you're about to discover how deep the rabbit hole goes and how crazy things get in Wonderland. This sentiment may appear an exaggeration, but slowly, you'll find it's anything but. The quantum universe really is that illogical. The rules of reality are anything but what they seem regarding quantum physics. Everything about the nature of reality will bend, boggle, befuddle, and blow your mind once you discover what quantum physics is about.

Imagine finding out your body is in two places or more at the same time, and that one version of yourself is over at Buckingham Palace racking your brain about how to remain relevant in this day and age, while another version of you is sipping a mai tai somewhere in Bali.

Picture flicking the light switch in your room on and off, and each time the light's on, your room is a different version of itself. Your wall paint, bed position, stuffed animals you're embarrassed to admit you still have, and the bazillion pillows are different every time. It sounds chaotic, doesn't it?

You know those socks of yours that mysteriously go missing? What if one of a pair is in Pluto and the other with you? Also, what if every time a Plutonian washes or dirties that sock, you can tell – *because your sock is a reflection of the alien's?* What does all this have to do with quantum physics?

First, you have to know the difference between classical physics and quantum physics. Classical physics is everything that pertains to the rules of the physical world as you perceive it with your five senses. It's stable and predictable. You know that if you throw a basketball in the air, it will return to Earth. Throw the ball hard against the floor, and it bounces. Pull a door open, and it moves toward you. Try to sit your ample bottom on a toddler's chair; with enough time and weight, it will break. Your bank is always at the same address, never moving from that spot, and the speed of light is fixed.

The laws of classical physics are fixed, unbreakable, and dependable, which is nice because how weird would it be to discover the sun now rises in the north or that the chair you're looking at in the corner isn't actually there right now? To put it formally, classical physics is a set of theoretical perspectives meant to explain observable phenomena and objects, such as planets, sound, light, cars, etc. The field of science studies the why and how of the movement of things, as well as how they work, unpacking the mechanics of magnetism, electricity, motion, sound, heat, gravity, and light.

Now you understand the basics of the classical version of physics, what about its quantum counterpart? Based on the introduction to the concept already offered, you're probably assuming it's nothing but the wild imagination of a fictional character in a cartoon – something cooked up in Dexter's Laboratory, perhaps. You'd be forgiven for thinking so. If quantum physics were a clock, the next minute after 7 AM would be 33:56 PM.

In other words, nothing quite lines up with the rules of classical physics. Depending on who's looking at it, one object is multiple things, all simultaneously. In this world, the speed of light isn't the fastest thing.

Okay, so you get the point and want a straightforward definition of quantum physics. Basically, **quantum physics is the field of science that studies the fundamentals of matter and energy, seeking to explain the universe at the level of atoms, electrons, and photons.**

The fact that you're reading this book means you've likely heard of quantum mechanics, too. Put simply, quantum mechanics is the mathematical language that describes the way atomic and subatomic particles move and interact with one another, working within frameworks like the uncertainty principle, correspondence principle, wave-particle duality, etc. Don't worry; these things will sound less like gibberish as you explore this quantum world further. In some contexts, quantum physics and quantum mechanics are used interchangeably.

Now, you could use a history lesson.

# Historical Context and Development of Quantum Theory

Before getting into anything else, credit must go where it's due. Max Planck was the one who came up with the quantum theory. Without him, the many other fascinating discoveries in this field may have remained forever unknown. This German physicist published a study that sent shockwaves through his field.

Max Planck came up with the quantum theory.¹

The study was about how radiation affects a "blackbody" substance, which is something that absorbs all light and energy with which it comes in contact. He found that there are times when energy acts like physical matter. According to classical physics, energy is only ever in the form of a wave. However, Planck had a theory that these waves actually had particles he dubbed *quanta*. He won the Nobel Prize for his groundbreaking work.

Albert Einstein built upon Planck's work. First, in 1905, he posited that light is actually made of particles. This was dismissed as preposterous at the time because everyone assumed that light was in *waveform*. He called light particles "photons" and stated that each one has energy within it.

Then, four years later, in 1909, Einstein shook the science world again with his wave-particle theory, stating that waves and particles can behave like one another, especially regarding electrons and photons. Why was this such a big deal? Well, if you read between the lines, he was essentially saying that a particle can act like a wave and a wave like a particle, *depending on how you look at them*. This was just one of several theories Einstein proved, even though he wasn't entirely a proponent of quantum mechanics, as he didn't like the idea of an uncertain reality. In his words, "God does not play dice."

*Sidenote:* Depending on whom you ask, Einstein actually got all his ideas from Mileva Marić, his wife, but because this was a time when women weren't acknowledged as much as they should have been for their brilliant minds, he got all the credit. This book isn't about that debate, so it's time to move on.

In 1913, Niels Bohr used the quantum concept to explain the structure of atoms and molecules. In his model, the nucleus is at the center of the atom, much like the sun is in the center of the known planets. The electrons are set up like planets around the nucleus, but their orbit doesn't stray beyond specific distances (called "energy levels") from their "sun."

In 1924, Louis de Broglie contributed to the quantum field of study by taking Einstein's original position even further. To Louis, light wasn't the only thing with the traits of waves and particles. He ascribed that property to everything in existence. In other words, simultaneously, everything can be a ball or an ocean wave. One must wonder what Einstein would have thought about that.

Werner Heisenberg would not only devise a different way to work out the math of quantum mechanics within the context of matrices but also introduce the world to his "Uncertainty Principle" in 1925. He might as well have said to Einstein, "God, in fact, *does* play dice."

There's no better analogy for his theory than a hummingbird in flight. Watch its wings, and you'll notice only one of two things: the speed at which the bird's wings beat against the air or the wings in a specific spot. You can only pick up on one or the other, not both simultaneously. This is a rather simplistic example, but it explains the weirdness of the Uncertainty Principle.

Of course, quantum physics wouldn't be what it is without the work of that one scientist who may or may not have had a cat at a certain point in his life. His name? Erwin Schrödinger. His Wave Theory of Matter validates Niels Bohr's insistence that God may fancy a game of roulette now and then. His eponymously named Schrödinger's Equation, formulated in 1926, offers a mathematical way to describe how the quantum state of a quantum system evolves over time.

Solutions derived from Erwin's equation offer an excellent way to tell what the probabilities of various outcomes may be, demonstrating clearly that a particle can exist in more states than you can count until you actually observe it, which fixes it to a single state – at least, while you're looking. If you're unfamiliar with Erwin's contributions, surely you know about Schrödinger's cat thought experiment. If you aren't, you will be soon enough!

Paul Dirac was another interesting character who took Einstein's Relativity Theory to a quantum level. You see, this particular theory of Einstein says that while the laws of physics work the same for everyone all over the world, what you observe may be different from what someone else observes, depending on the direction of the movement of an object and its speed.

So, Dirac took this theory and applied it to the quantum world. He developed the Dirac Equation, which demonstrated how electrons and similar particles act whenever their movement approaches the speed of light. The man was able to predict that antimatter was a real thing. What's that? Antimatter is the mirrored version of matter, having the *opposite energetic charge.*

In 1932, Carl D. Anderson validated Paul's assumption that antimatter exists, thanks to his discovery of the positron as he was looking into the behavior of particles with a high energy charge known as cosmic rays from space. As he tracked the particles using his cloud chamber device, he noticed certain tracks left behind by said particles that appeared to be similar in mass to the electron – but positively charged instead. When he experimented with shooting high-energy light or gamma rays into various materials, he proved conclusively that each electron is paired with a positron.

One more honorable mention is Richard Feynman, who did phenomenal work on Quantum Electrodynamics or QED, which offers clarity on the interaction between electrons (matter) and photons (light). He created the Feynman diagrams, which acted as roadmaps to show how this interaction evolves over time, making handling all the complex calculations in QED much easier.

Not only that, but the brilliant Feynman devised a simple way to work out all the possible ways a particle can journey from one point to another. It's like knowing every

Richard Feynman.[8]

possible path that the ants that have been bothering you at home could make, from their nest to the cake sitting on your kitchen counter, including the illogical paths. Feynman's work also made quantum computing and nanotechnology possible, and he took it upon himself to teach physics principles to laypeople, breaking complex ideas into simple forms, much like this book does.

## The Cornerstones of Quantum Physics

So . . . the bell has rung, and history class is over. Now, it's time to explore the different theories that, together, make up the fabric of quantum physics. Don't worry; you'll get clear explanations that won't make you want to gouge your eyes out.

**Quantum Field Theory:** Also called QFT, this theory combines quantum mechanics principles, which govern the nature of subatomic particles, with relativity, which is about everything to do with large distances and high speeds. Thanks to QFT, everyone now understands how subatomic particles interact through various force fields. Think of the world as being a giant ocean of energy. Particles such as photons and electrons act as ripples or waves in this universal energetic ocean. What's causing the ripples? Energy itself.

So, according to the Quantum Field Theory, the particles act as excitations that cause rippling waves that occur in their underlying fields. What are these underlying fields? Think of them as energetic blankets all over the universe. There is a separate blanket (field) for each kind of particle. When you pick a point in a field and add energy to it, the energy causes a disturbance or ripple, which is the particle itself.

**String Theory:** According to this theoretical framework, particles aren't simply infinitesimally small points or dots in space as depicted in regular physics, but more like the tiniest pieces of string. The strings can vibrate, and how they vibrate determines the particle's mass, energetic charge, and other unique traits. So, this theory looks into how these strings travel through space and how they affect one another in the process.

One of many visual interpretations of string theory.'

There are various vibrational states these strings can be in, one of the most important ones being the graviton. The graviton is a particle governed by quantum mechanics that contains the gravitational force, and this is why string theory is also known as quantum gravity theory. It is an all-encompassing theory that explains everything in the universe using the language of mathematics, describing every force in existence and matter in all its forms, known and unknown.

One implication of this theory is that there are other universes besides the one you know, which operate by different laws of physics, and that there are other dimensions beyond what is known about time and space that remain imperceptible – for now. If you think that's crazy, try this on for size: If string theory is correct, that would mean the universe is actually a hologram. Is a sense of existential crisis looming in your mind? You may want to hold off on that for now.

**Wave-Particle Duality:** This concept suggests that all particles can act as both waves and particles. Think of light. Focus it on a surface, and its photoelectric effect can knock the object's electrons loose, which shows that light can act like a particle. It is like when you're playing pool, and the white cue ball strikes another ball to make it move. The other ball moves because the white ball transfers energy to it once it makes contact, and, in the context of light hitting a surface, it also causes movement by knocking electrons out of place.

If you take that same light and let it shine through a narrow slit, guess what? It acts like a wave because it will cause an interference pattern. What's that? It's the light forming a pattern of light and dark bands, which is something waves do. You can understand this by thinking of the ripples of waves created when you drop a pebble into a pond. Light can be wavy, too. It's the same thing for other forms of matter, like electrons. As particles, they can move from one specific spot to another, but as waves, they spread out, so they aren't tied down to one location but are in multiple places at once.

**Quantum Superposition:** This is a quantum mechanics concept that states all particles exist in more than one state simultaneously unless and until someone observes them. Remember Schrödinger's cat? Well, the science behind that is that it's attention and observation that fixes the position and state of a particle.

Particles are in a superposition, which means multiple positions. They're not moving around these positions but are in every one. Have you ever heard your kooky New Age friend say something like, "There's only here and now?" Well, this concept is the scientific way to explain that. It suggests that particles act like all that exists is here and now, at least until you pay some attention to them! When you do, they'll pick a spot.

**Quantum Entanglement:** This quantum mechanics concept is one where a pair of particles become connected to each other, so even if they're the furthest they could be from each other, whatever changes one of them experiences will be reflected in the other – and that's why your nonexistent sock from earlier in this book keeps washing and dirtying itself.

To put it in scientific, non-sock terms, when you know the measurements of a particle, you know the same of the other particle. Now, you may think that surely, at some point in space beyond a certain distance, the connection between these particles must be broken. After all, isn't that kind of how WiFi works? Head outside and walk far enough from the house, and you'll lose the connection to the network at home, right?

Well, that's not quite it.

These linked particles could be lightyears apart, yet they'll still mirror each other because they're entangled. Einstein referred to this as "spooky action at a distance." That's a fitting description of quantum entanglement, and if you think about it, that explains why certain spiritual practices require "sympathetic magic," where practitioners like Voodooists, for instance, use items to represent the people they'd like to help or hex.

**The Uncertainty Principle:** Also called Heisenberg's Uncertainty Principle, this concept states there's no way to be aware of a particle's location and precise speed as it moves in a specific direction *simultaneously*. You can only know one or the other. When you can track the location precisely, you won't be able to do the same for its speed, and vice versa. What gives? Are scientific instruments pointless? No, that's not the case. This is simply the way quantum particles operate. It's as if their principle is the meme, "Never let them know your next move."

**Quantum Tunneling:** If you throw a ball against the wall, you expect the wall to stop it in its tracks, right? Also, if you roll that same ball down a hill, you expect it to keep going, right? In quantum physics, there is a concept called quantum tunneling, which would suggest that rather than the ball being stopped by the wall or going over the hill, it would pass through both obstacles.

So, you can see that this theory would not work in classical physics because if you attempt to drive a car through a barrier like a gate, it will lead to a terrible accident. However, quantum tunneling occurs frequently in quantum physics, as particles move or "tunnel" through obstacles or barriers, like a hot knife through nonexistent butter.

## Quantum Physics, Applied

There are numerous ways quantum physics can be applied in modern technology. Here's a quick overview of some of them. First, consider lasers. These work using stimulated emission. In simple English, a light particle (photon) is used to cause a reaction or "stimulate" an already excited electron, causing its energy state to drop lower, resulting in the release of two photons that are similar in nature, giving you a powerful, concentrated light beam. This entire process relies on quantum physics.

What about transistors? Modern electronics, as you know them, wouldn't exist without them, which would be a bummer. The transistors are the cornerstone of all electronics, and they work with the principle of quantum mechanics, which is how electricity flows where it should through circuits.

Even the world of medicine benefits from quantum physics. Magnetic Resonance Imaging (or MRI) machines are necessary to diagnose the problems patients deal with since they offer a clear snapshot of what's going on inside the body. Magnetic Resonance Imaging works with quantum physics. How? This imaging technique is made possible by controlling how atomic nuclei spin and picking up on the resulting radio waves when the nuclei go back to their actual state.

Then there's cryptography, which is necessary to ensure no third party can decipher messages sent end-to-end. If you get a message, you're the only one who can read it, and no one else can. There's research going on in the security field that's working to incorporate quantum principles into the cryptography process. How?

Remember the Uncertainty Principle? If someone observes a particle, its behavior will change. In quantum cryptography, if an eavesdropper is trying to get in between you and your message when it's transmitted to you, the original message will be altered significantly, and this alerts you and the sender to the fact that one of you has a personal FBI agent assigned to them.

## Things to Remember

1. In quantum physics, energy isn't some nebulous thing that cannot be measured. It occurs in discrete units.
2. Particles also act as waves.
3. Particles exist in several states at the same time.
4. Two particles can become linked, mirroring each other no matter their distance.
5. There's no way to tell the speed and location of a particle with precision.
6. Particles can move through various potential energy constraints, which is something classical physics insists is an impossibility.
7. Schrödinger's cat is really an explanation of superposition and doesn't mean your cat dies every time you can't find it.

# Chapter 2: Exploring Particle Behavior

Now you've been introduced to the wacky world of quantum physics, what's next? In this chapter, it is time to dive into the behavior of particles, both as waves and particles on the quantum level.

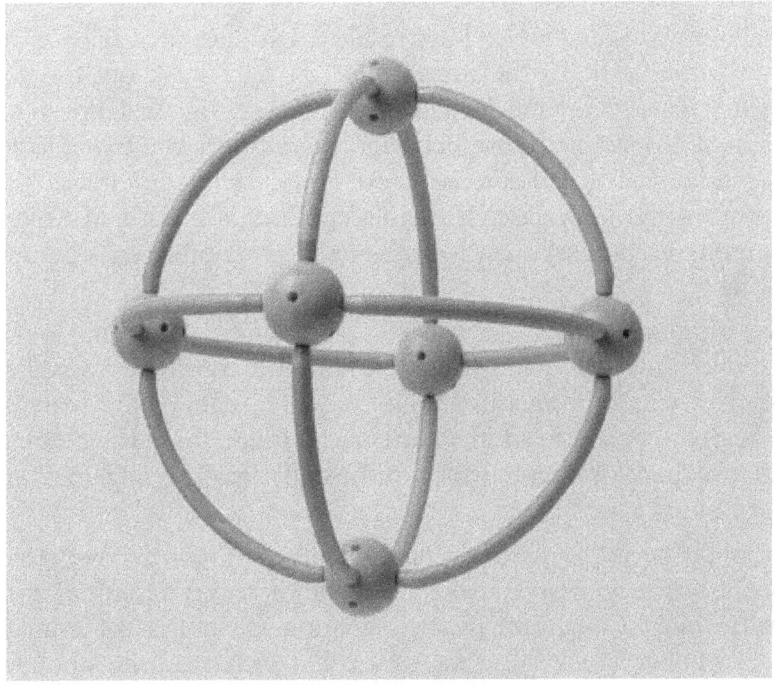

Particles on the quantum level.[5]

# Classical Particles Versus Quantum Particles

If you're going to get this quantum physics thing down, it's essential to know the difference between the way particles behave in the quantum framework versus the classical one. You already know some of this based on what you've learned from the previous chapter, but it doesn't hurt to go over them once more to be thorough.

Deterministic behavior versus probabilistic behavior: When it comes to classical physics, you can determine how a particle is going to act in the future once you understand its current state. That's why it's known as deterministic. There are rules, and all the rules are respected. When you know the speed at which a planet moves and its present position, you can work out where it will be at a later date with little to no wiggle room for error. Classical physics has to do with macroscopic objects – as in objects large enough for you to observe with the *naked eye.*

On the flip side, quantum physics involves microscopic objects, and in this world, probability reigns supreme because nothing is definite. What's 1 plus 1? It's probably 2, 20, or a zebra. That's because quantum particles live in a world with multiple possibilities that are all dependent on wave functions.

What are wave functions? They're like road maps that tell you how to find the particle. Here's the thing. You can only work out the odds of finding the particle in one location over others, but that doesn't mean you've pinned down its future behavior. Think of it like trying to predict where smoke will go. There are too many factors to track, so your prediction will be imprecise. If classical physics is black and white, then quantum physics is every shade of gray – and every other color known and unknown.

Fixed location or momentum versus uncertainty: According to classical physics, every particle has a fixed location and travels at a fixed speed. This is why you can measure them precisely. Generally, macroscopic objects tend to remain fixed in a particular position, and when they aren't, then they're in movement, which means they're traveling in a specific trajectory and at a set speed.

The opposite is the case in quantum physics, where every particle is potentially a wave as well. So, in classical physics, you'd think of a particle as a ball, while in quantum physics, it would be more like a wave or a plume of smoke. There is no way you could pick out "one smoke" from that plume, and if you could, that would be an awesome trick to see!

One reason trying to measure both the position and speed of a particle in quantum physics is a fool's errand is because the very act of observing it or attempting to measure it would cause a disturbance in its momentum and vice versa.

Single state versus superposition: You already know what superposition is, so there's no need to bore you with the details. However, it is important to know that superposition is a concept that only applies to quantum physics and not classical physics. In classical physics, a particle can only be in one location at any given time.

To help you understand this better, imagine that you have a coin. The coin should have two sides to it: heads and tails. If you flip that coin and it lands, it can only land on heads or tails. Sure, you could probably pull off a trick shot and let it land on its side, but that's not what this is about, so don't be cheeky. Even if it did land on its side, the point is in classical physics, your coin would be on its side only, not on its side, heads, and tails, as would be the case in quantum physics.

Independence versus entanglement: Now you have two coins (you're a real Mr. Moneybags, aren't you?) Flip both coins simultaneously, and the odds are that they *will* land. However, they will land independently of each other. Whether they both land on heads or tails or land on different sides, it all comes down to the starting conditions before you flipped the coins and other factors that may have affected them as they turned in the air and landed on the ground. This is how it works in classical physics. Neither coin affects the other. Every particle, according to classical physics, is independent.

However, in quantum physics, those coins can develop a connection, or a sort of "energetic chemistry," if you will. Whether your coins are in the same room with you or galaxies apart, they affect each other. So if you're getting heads when you flip your coin, whoever has the other coin is also getting heads. In quantum physics, these coins (particles) are entangled. Thanks to Einstein's "spooky action at a distance," both coins are connected with each other and can communicate with each other.

Now, granted, the example with the coins is a little bit simplistic because the thing about particles in quantum physics is that while the entangled particles' fates affect one another, it is impossible to predict what will happen to them in the future after or while attempting to measure them.

Continuous energy spectrum versus discrete energy levels: Think about how you can gradually increase or decrease the volume of your TV, or think about a dimmer switch and how you can gradually reduce or increase the brightness in your room. You see, according to classical physics, you can add or remove energy in infinitesimally small amounts to cause smooth motion.

According to classical physics, there is no limit to the amount of energy that can be contained within a particle. However, according to quantum physics, each particle has discrete energy levels which are distinct and measurable. What does this mean? As you switch from one level of energy to another, in classical physics, the movement is smooth and continuous. That's not the case in quantum physics because each particle has a discrete energy level. It jumps from one level to another.

Now, come back to the dimmer switch analogy. The particle can go straight from light to darkness and back. The dimmer switch wouldn't be a *dimmer switch* as the particles teleport from dark to light right away rather than through a gradual increase of light. This is why neon signs have a vibrant glow as you watch the electrons teleport around to create it.

## Diving Deeper into Wave-Particle Duality

While you've already been introduced to the concept of wave-particle duality, there's much more to explore. In 1928, Niels Bohr developed his complementarity principle, which posits that the only way to truly understand quantum phenomena is by being fully conversant with the properties of waves and particles. You could set up an experiment that would cause photons and electrons to act like waves. Make a few tweaks to your setup, and the next thing you know, these particles are acting like particles instead.

But how can you tell the difference between the two? When a quantum particle is being a particle, it can

Niels Bohr.[6]

dislodge electrons from surfaces. You see this play out in the photoelectric effect, which was discovered by your favorite white-haired genius, Albert Einstein, in 1905. So here's a breakdown. Think of light as a continuous flowing wave, much like the ripples in a lake or a pond.

According to classical physics, when there is a gradual increase in the brightness or wave intensity, you expect there to be a corresponding gradual increase in the energy that is transferred onto the electrons of, say, a metal surface. However, it wouldn't matter how bright the light gets. That wouldn't be enough to cause electrons to be ejected from the surface.

After a few tests, Einstein realized that no matter how strong the light is, it will always eject electrons from a metal surface if the energy frequency is above a certain threshold. Put differently, if you had the brightest light and its frequency wasn't high enough, the electrons would remain in place.

However, if the light is weak, it can cause electron emission if its frequency is high. The only particles capable of dislodging electrons are the photons that have energy beyond the metal's work function, which is the least amount of energy you'd need to trigger electron emission.

On the flip side, when photons and electrons act like waves, they can interfere with one another, and it's this interference that leads to light patterns and dark bands reminiscent of a rippling pond.

Now, bring your attention back to the complementarity principle. This principle makes it clear that you cannot observe the particle traits and wave traits of a particle at the same time. Nevertheless, you have to consider both of them simultaneously to be able to describe them fully since they complement each other. Wave-particle duality is a particularly useful concept when it comes to photonics, electron microscopy, quantum computing, and semiconductor devices, among other applications.

## More on Superposition

As you've discovered, particles in quantum physics are never in a definite state unless and until you observe them. For instance, if you like to play the lottery, it's like having a ticket and not scratching it yet. Until the point when you scratch it, it remains both a winning and a losing ticket. A particle like an electron is here *and* there, but when you finally observe it, it chooses to be here *or* there. This isn't witchcraft. This is a concept that has been proven with laboratory experiments using electrons. You'll learn more about a famous experiment called the *double-slit experiment* in a later chapter.

The concept of superposition can also be found in quantum computing. A bit is the smallest unit of information that is used in computing. When it comes to quantum computing, the bits are called quantum bits or qubits. In this context, the qubit can be in both 0 and 1 states (remember, computers work with the binary of 0 and 1).

It is this ability that makes it possible for a quantum computer to outperform regular computers, as they're able to solve the most complex calculations you could imagine at record-breaking speed. The minute you give attention to a quantum system, it will be forced to pick one of the possible states available. This process is called a **wave function collapse**. Once it fixes itself to a state, every other possibility becomes nonexistent.

Superposition completely rips apart the ideas of determinism and locality, cornerstones of classical physics. This is one of the reasons that classical physicists are opposed to quantum physics. Who could blame them? After all, it is a little scary to think the universe's future cannot be predicted. If there's one thing most people fear, it's the unknown. Also, can you imagine a world where nothing is fixed in place?

Imagine inviting a friend over for brunch. They ask you when they should show up, and you tell them to come by 12:00 PM two years from now or by 5:00 PM three weeks ago.

They ask you for your address, and you tell them it's *probably* on the corner of Diagon Alley and 6th Avenue and probably in Sector 12 on the dark side of the moon. They'll need all the luck they can get to find an Uber to get them there, and if Rolex can figure out how to create a quantum wristwatch, they'd make a killing!

All this is to say that when it comes to superposition, the definite does not exist. Without the observer effect (the phenomenon where your attention on a particle fixes it in space and time), it's all in a haze of probabilities.

## Into the Quantum Tunnel

The theory of quantum tunneling has already been explained in the previous chapter. In classical physics, when you throw a baseball against the wall, it will bounce back. That ball can't pass through the wall unless, of course, it's the platform 9 ¾ in the "Potterverse." It's also impossible for that ball to make its way over the hill unless you put enough kinetic energy behind it to get it moving.

When it comes to quantum physics, quantum tunneling is a thing. The tunneling particle doesn't need "enough" energy to get through obstacles. How is this even possible? In quantum physics, you talk about particles in the context of wave functions, which are mathematical functions that explain the probability of locating a specific particle in various locations.

Every time a particle comes face to face with an obstacle or barrier, the wave function will go down dramatically, but never so low as to hit zero while it is within the obstacle. Since there's a nonzero probability of finding the particle on the opposite side of the barrier, this is what allows the particle to make a tunnel through it.

Is this starting to sound a little too much like gibberish? Well put simply, nonzero probability means a "tiny chance." The wave function is basically a cloud or a plume of smoke that surrounds the particle. If you have a particularly dense cloud, you are likely to find the particle within it.

A dramatic decrease in the wave function means that the cloud would become thinner and thinner as you move further into the barrier that obstructs the particle. The thinner that cloud is, the less likely you will find the particle in it. Now, just because the wave function has decreased doesn't mean it totally disappears when it's within the barrier or obstacle, which gives the particle that "slim chance" or nonzero probability of popping up on the other side.

## Particle Collisions

Every particle has its unique field. The fields make it possible for particles to connect with one another. Look at electrons, for instance. Their interaction involves the exchange of virtual photons, which are different from regular ones. Regular photons are the particles you can pick up on as electromagnetic radiation or light, while virtual photons are mathematical tools you use in quantum physics to explain how charged particles interact with one another. They're "virtual" because there's no way to directly observe them, and they are used to hold all sorts of energies - including energies that aren't physical.

There's no way to understand the quantum world fully without knowing about particle collision, which is a term to explain the way particles interact. These collisions last a short period and could be between subatomic particles such as protons and electrons- or larger ones like molecules and atoms.

There are three kinds of collisions: elastic, inelastic, and perfectly inelastic. In elastic collisions, the speed (momentum) and kinetic energy (the energy required to make the particles move) are conserved in the process. The inelastic collisions will conserve the momentum but not the kinetic energy. As for the perfectly inelastic collisions, after the particles have collided, they remain stuck together.

Scientists look at these interactions to better understand the laws of the quantum world, and they work with particle accelerators like the Large Hadron Collider at CERN to learn more. Devices like these basically cause the particles to move at high speeds and then bump up against one another with enough force to form new particles that can be studied. This process is how the Higgs boson particle was discovered. This particle is unique because it's responsible for giving mass to other particles.

## The "Okay, Buts" of Quantum Physics

So, you understand the basics of quantum physics, but what gives? Surely, certain concepts won't fit into the box of quantum physics, right? Well, you're correct in that assumption. To wrap up this chapter, here are some of the challenges with this branch of physics:

1. The fact that quantum mechanics and physics are about studying the microscopic universe makes it difficult for many to relate to, and it certainly doesn't help that many of the discoveries and theories in this field do not fit in with common sense.
2. Particular aspects of quantum physics are still quite a challenge to apply in the real, macroscopic world, especially when it comes to technology.
3. In practice, superposition eventually breaks down into a state of decoherence where the particle that was "everything, everywhere, all at once" is now just the one thing in one state in the present. Superposition could be a boon to quantum computing as soon as some genius figures out how to halt the decoherence process.

## Still Elusive

A few aspects of particle behavior are still under review in quantum physics. For instance, some particles have memory, as they're able to keep track of their pasts. These are called *non-abelian anyons*, and research on them has been going on for decades now. Then, there's another set of particles known as *neutrinos*. As they travel through space, they can change from one type or "flavor" of a particle to another, oscillating from one of three flavors to another as they move. They could be electron neutrinos, muon neutrinos, or tau neutrinos. Finally, certain metals are anything but conventional, having high-energy particles that may hold some promise in helping scientists find a new way to craft detectors that can pick up on wavelengths scientific instruments can't detect right now.

# Chapter 3: What is Light?

Now, it's time to talk about light. You may not realize it, but there's so much more to light than just "light," you know? You'll learn more about it in this chapter as you discover the quantum theory of light, which explains how it behaves when you study it from a quantum level.

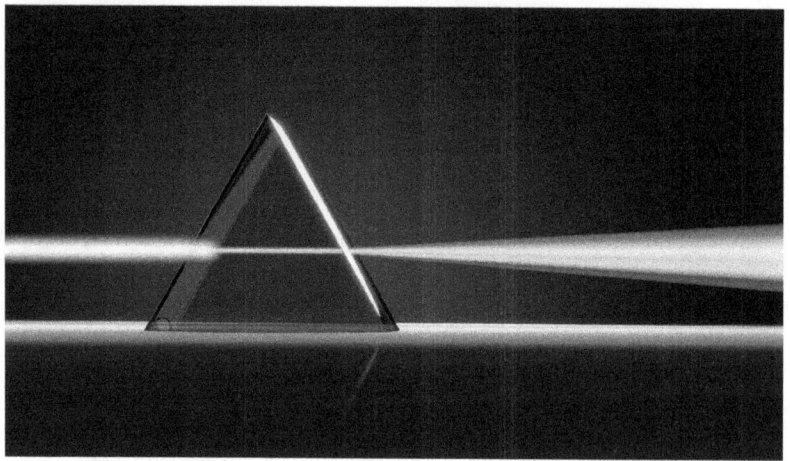

Discover the quantum theory of light.[7]

## From Classical Optics to Quantum Optics

You can't talk about light without talking about optics. But what do "optics" mean in the first place? Classical optics is an aspect of physics that seeks to offer a comprehensive description of light, with the perspective that light rays move through space in straight lines through objects that are large enough for you to see with your eyes with no special instrument.

In this branch of optics, scientists are curious to know how light makes its way through glass, water, air, and other macroscopic media like those. Every time light passes through these media, it doesn't do so quietly. If you could observe the molecules and atoms of the medium, you'd notice the light doing a lot of magic. For instance, it bends when it has to go from one medium to another through the process of refraction. Sometimes, it bounces to create a reflection; other times, it's absorbed by the medium.

What about quantum optics? This is an aspect of AMO physics, Atomic, Molecular, and Optical Physics, which is about how light interacts with quantum matter. You're definitely going to need special instruments to observe light in action because human eyes can't pick up on quantum information – at least not yet. Perhaps that's something that will change with newer iterations of Elon Musk's Neuralink.

Quantum physicists look at light differently. Ask one, and they'll tell you it's made of photons, which are discrete packets of energy. What do they mean by "discrete," though? Is it a "secret light?" You'd be forgiven for thinking that. These photons are "discrete," not "discreet," in the sense that each of these energy packets has fixed attributes and measurements. Their traits are defined rather than on a spectrum, which is why these packets are known as quanta (because they're "quantized").

The energy in a photon can only be in certain multiples of a basic unit, which you can work out using Planck's constant (h) and the light's frequency (f) using the formula $E=hf$.

Here, dear reader, lies the key difference between classical and quantum optics. In the former, energy can be assigned any value and exists in a continuous range rather than being discrete or quantized. Also, quantum optics honors the principles of quantum mechanics, which, as you know, do not jive well with classical physics. The essence of quantum optics is to help everyone understand the kooky, spooky stuff that goes on with light at the quantum level.

So here's a summary of the differences between both fields of optics. The classical view of optics holds that light occurs in continuous waves, while quantum optics sees light as individual particles called photons, with the ability to exhibit wave-like behavior, in line with the wave-particle duality of quantum physics.

Classical optics holds that any value can be taken on or assigned to light, whether that's in terms of momentum, energy, or other quantities, while quantum optics insists on discretion in light's values. One more thing quantum physics considers to be true of light is the entanglement theory. It posits that the light particles can and do become linked to each other so that they mirror each other regardless of how much space is between them.

It would be remiss to talk about quantum optics without touching on Quantum Electrodynamics or QED, the relativistic quantum field theory of electrodynamics. In case you feel that the previous sentence might as well have been summarized as "gobbledygook," here's a breakdown of what that means.

You already know quantum field theory is the study of the interactions between particles. Electrodynamics is about taking a closer look at *electrically charged* particles, in particular, and watching how they interact with light. As for the word "relativistic," it's from Einstein's theory of relativity, which, if you remember, states that no matter how fast you go, the laws of physics and the speed of light will remain constant for everyone and everything observing you.

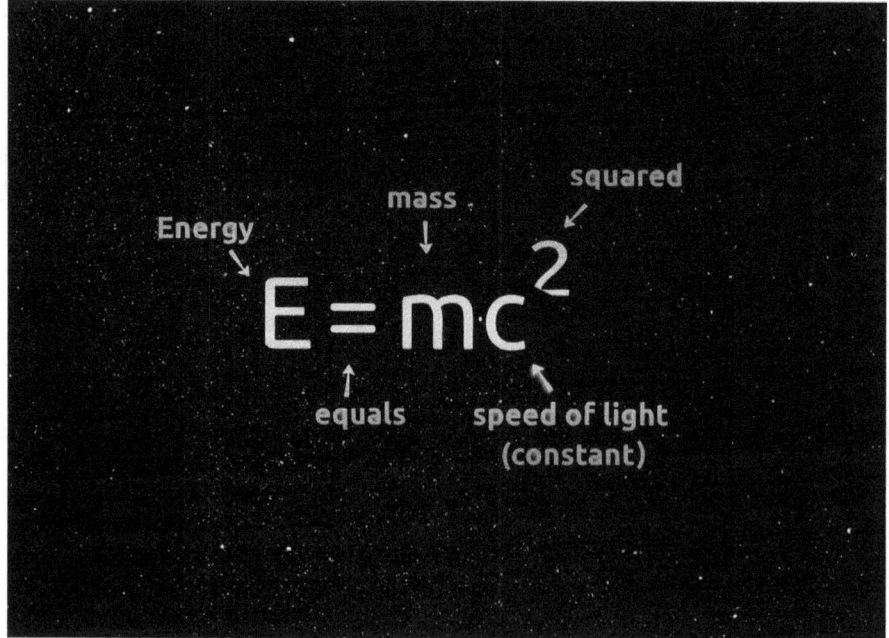

Einstein's theory of relativity states that no matter how fast you go, the laws of physics and the speed of light will remain constant for everyone and everything observing you.'

Now, putting all that together, QED is a combo of studying the smallest of things (quantum mechanics) and the fastest of things (special relativity) to illuminate how matter and light interact with one another.

**Interesting side note:** This theory is the very first of the lot in the quantum field, and it actually aligns well with Einstein's relativity theory. Using the language of mathematics, QED describes everything that happens with electrically charged particles as they exchange photons, and it's the quantum answer to classical electromagnetism.

According to quantum electrodynamics, the interaction between photons and matter (also called "coupling") concerns an energy exchange between both. It is a coherent process, meaning both matter and light are within the same frequency and phase, making it possible for the energy exchange to occur without any loss - and without it dying out or dissipating.

To make that simpler to understand, think of what "incoherent" interactions might imply - in this scenario, as energy is exchanged, it is lost as radiation or heat. Now, back to the matter of coherent energetic exchange between light and matter. In QED, particles on both sides have the same energy and momentum.

Now, there are four fundamental forces of nature.
1. **Gravity:** The force that pulls two objects together as long as they have energy or mass. Gravity also happens to be the weakest of the four forces, but it makes up for that weakness with the fact that there's not one thing in all the universe that isn't affected by it.
2. **Electromagnetism:** Then there's electromagnetism, which is what you find between electrically charged particles and create magnetic and electric fields. Unlike gravity, electromagnetism doesn't have as much range, and if you want to cancel it out, all you need are opposite charges, and it's over.
3. **Strong Nuclear Force:** Next, there's the strong nuclear force responsible for keeping a neutron and proton bound with the nucleus of an atom. It isn't called "strong" for nothing, as it's the most powerful of the four natural forces.
4. **Weak Nuclear Force:** Finally, there's the weak nuclear force which leads to nuclear fusion and radioactive decay and is only found with subatomic particles. According to the classical point of view, light and matter are seen as distinct things, and light is only ever seen as a wave. However, according to QED, light and matter are seen as unified.

# The Pioneers of QED

Who are the brilliant minds who pioneered this quantum field theory, and what did they contribute? Well, you already know about **Paul Dirac**, who was the first person to come up with the quantum theory of radiation and matter interaction. He also came up with the term "quantum electrodynamics," which he shared with the world in 1928. Dirac worked out the mathematical equation explaining what was going on with the movement of electrons and how they spin. He dubbed his explanation "the wave equation."

Next up was **Enrico Fermi**. Enrico came up with a brilliant formulation of Quantum Electrodynamics in 1932. How? He worked with the idea of virtual particles, using them to clarify how charged particles interact with light particles. Other honorable mentions are **Felix Bloch, Arnold Nordsieck, and Victor Weisskopf,** who would shed light on the problem physicists constantly came up against when it came to infinities in higher-order calculations.

Enrico Fermi [9]

Yes, you want that broken down, don't you? You remember QED is about the interaction between light and matter at the quantum level, right? Well, physicists only predict these interactions through the lens of the perturbation theory, which you can think of as making a series of approximate calculations that become more accurate with each new iteration.

These three scientists found out that the perturbation theory was sorely lacking. You see, each time they wanted more accurate approximations, they would only wind up with answers that didn't add up. The answers were infinite, and that's why that phenomenon is called "the problem of infinities," which meant QED couldn't be trusted because it lacked consistency and, therefore, couldn't be relied upon.

So, Bloch and Nordsieck came together to figure out this problem and discover something to help them skirt around the infinities issue in a specific context. In this situation, when the charged particles emitted significantly low-energy light, the infinities would be canceled out, which meant that scientists' predictions could match their experiments. This solution is known as the Bloch-Nordsieck Theorem.

As for Weisskopf, he worked on his own and discovered there was another unique instance that allows you to avoid the problem of infinities: when the charged particles absorb light, that happens to be higher energy.

Was the problem of infinities ever sorted out? Yes. In the late 1940s, **Richard Feynman, Julian Schwinger, and Shin'ichiro Tomonaga** would independently come up with a solution, developing a version of QED that was dependable and accurate. Feynman offered his diagrams, Schwinger developed the action principle, and Tomonaga shared his ideas on renormalization. Feynman's diagrams are drawings showing how photons and electrons interact with one another by swapping photons, and they mathematically depict the odds of these particles interacting in a specific way. His diagrams work because he assigned some of them with a negative sign, which meant that after summing them all up, the infinities were canceled out, leaving behind answers that made sense.

Schwinger's action principle says that when you have a physical system, its action, which is a quantity physicists use to measure how said system changes over time, will always be the smallest or largest value possible. This rule helped him explain the movements and fields in QED. That's not all Schwinger came up with, though. Using a method he dubbed "regularization," he found you could add a small number to the values to force the infinities to become finite, and then at the end of the calculation, he'd eliminate that same number.

Tomonaga's renormalization is another interesting method centered around the fact that when it comes to the numbers in Quantum Electrodynamics, such as the values for the electron's charge and mass, those figures are never fixed. Instead, they're in a state of flux, and their value depends on how small or how fast these traits are measured. So, Tomonaga would use his method to switch the numbers around to eliminate the infinities.

## The Photoelectric Effect and the Compton Effect

This is a chapter about light, so it makes sense to talk about the photoelectric effect. What's that about? It's when the light leads to the ejection of electrons from a metal's surface, which was first noticed by Heinrich Hertz in 1887. This phenomenon was not explained until Albert Einstein offered an explanation in 1905.

Through the lens of classical physics, light is a wave that can have any amount of energy depending on how quickly it vibrates and how intensely or brightly it shines. The assumption was that the number of electrons ejected (and their energy) came down to these two factors, *but experiments proved otherwise.* What did experiments demonstrate?

1. The intensity of the light determined how many electrons would be emitted. In this case, more intense means more electrons.
2. The electrons' energy is a matter of the light's frequency. So, if the light has a shorter wavelength or higher frequency, the electrons emitted would have more energy.
3. There is a specific threshold below which no electrons can be ejected. This is the case when the light has a longer wavelength or lower frequency. Also, its brightness is not a factor at all.
4. Finally, the electron ejection process happens the moment the light connects with the metal. You know how you'd expect to hold a blade over the fire for a while before it finally gets hot? Well, that's not how it works when light hits metal because the emission is instant.

Einstein figured the results were what they were, thanks to the fact that light is a stream of photons, each with a set amount of energy determined by its frequency. The formula he came up with to explain a photon's energy is $E = hf$, with E being energy, f being frequency, and h being Planck's constant, which has already been discussed.

Einstein also posited that each photon could only transfer energy to just one electron, and not only that, but the metal also needed a work function (a set amount of energy) to eject an electron. His formula for working out the kinetic energy contained in a single electron emitted by the metal is $KE = hf - W$, with KE being kinetic energy, f being frequency, h being Planck's constant, and W being the work function.

The photoelectric effect shows the truth about light being able to act as a wave and a particle and the fact that light's energy must be quantized. It also demonstrates that light and matter do not interact with each other continuously and smoothly – but probabilistically.

Now that's out of the way, it's essential to focus on the Compton Effect, eponymously named after Arthur Compton. This effect was first observed in 1923. Arthur found that light can change its frequency (color) or wavelength and scatter off electrons, demonstrating that light truly acts as a particle.

Classical physics always assumed that scattered light would have the same frequency as incident light. To be clear, scattered light is the light that is produced as a result of bouncing off the electrons, while incident light is the light before the bounce happens. Classical physics was proven wrong once more, as experiments showed that:

1. The frequency of scattered light is much lower than that of the incident light. In other words, it has the lower frequency of the two lights.
2. The wavelength or frequency changes depending on the angle at which the scattering occurs. So, if the angle is larger, you can expect larger changes, and the smaller the angle, the smaller the changes.
3. These frequency changes have nothing to do with the light's intensity.

Arthur Compton confirmed the theory of light being a stream of photons. To understand the Compton Effect visually, scattered light will have a redder hue than the incident light. How does this play out? First, the photon strikes the electron, and in the process, the former gives some of its momentum and energy to the latter, causing the electrons to move faster and the photon to lose its own momentum and energy. So, you'll notice the photon losing its blue hue and looking more like red.

Arthur Compton confirmed the theory of light being a stream of photons.[10]

## Quantum States, Coherent States, and Squeezed States

Think of quantum states as mathematical explanations of the different results you get when you measure systems like photons, molecules, or atoms to track variables like spin, polarization, energy, etc. Quantum states are represented with symbols known as kets or ket vectors. You could write the quantum states of physical systems using combos of simpler states, also called *basis states*. These basis states have a set value for each property being measured.

A photon with zero energy is written as |0>. If it has 1 unit of energy, it's written as |1>. Another way to write out a photon's quantum state is by using a combo of two other kinds of basis states, where the photon is horizontally polarized (|+>) or vertically polarized (|->). There's also the photon being written with the basis states \L> and |R>, which stand for the photon either having a left circular polarization or a right one, respectively.

One thing to note about quantum states is you can't know all the traits of a physical system simultaneously because of the uncertainty principle. Also, as a system's quantum state interacts with its environment or other systems, it changes with time. This change is worked out using the

Schrödinger equation. The very process of measuring anything about a system is enough to change its quantum state, forcing it to collapse into or select one of the basis states. Which one? It's impossible to predict, at least for now.

So, when you're considering the quantum state of light, you'll learn about the probabilities you'll get from measuring its properties, and you won't be able to predict the wave-function collapse. Some quantum states are more useful or meaningful than others, like coherent states, squeezed states, and entangled states.

**Coherent states** are quantum states of light with special traits. They never fluctuate in time because their phase and amplitude remain constant. Their shape and size remain the same over time, and so do their direction and color. So, light in coherent states can't blend in with other colors. Also, coherent states are harmonious, meaning they will blend well with other photons or waves of light.

Look at lasers, for instance. (Laser is the acronym for "Light Amplification by Stimulated Emission of Radiation.") The stimulated emission is a quantum process. This is when a photon stimulates or excites a molecule or atom with the same energy to create a new photon with the same energy level, direction, phase, and frequency. The photons that are created are all the same and coherent. These coherent states make tracking the light's phase easier, which matters in measurement methods like metrology, spectroscopy, and interferometry.

Lasers are created when a photon stimulates or excites a molecule or atom with the same energy.[11]

**Entangled states** can be generated by coherent states, too. Entangled states are quantum states where two or more physical systems are inexplicably correlated to each other, and these states are excellent for making advancements in the fields of quantum computation, communication, and information.

**Squeeze states** are quantum light states that have a lower uncertainty in one trait of light versus another to which it's specially related. These states can be created using mirrors, fibers, crystals, and other similar materials. The benefit of light in a squeezed state is that you can use it for far more precise measurements, better cryptography, faster computation, and more.

So, now that you understand everything about optics according to quantum physics, it's time to dive into the various quantum experiments that shaped the field of quantum physics. You'll get detailed explanations of the experimental setups, procedures, and observed outcomes.

# Chapter 4: Quantum Observations, Experiments, and Their Interpretations

In this chapter, you'll learn more about some of the most famous quantum experiments that have led to the current state of quantum physics.

## Young's Double-Slit Experiment (1801)

Young's Double-Slit Experiment demonstrated that light acts like a wave. Before Young pulled off this groundbreaking experiment, there were two tenets that scientists held onto strongly when it came to light: the corpuscular theory, which Isaac Newton postulated, and Christiaan Huygens's wave theory.

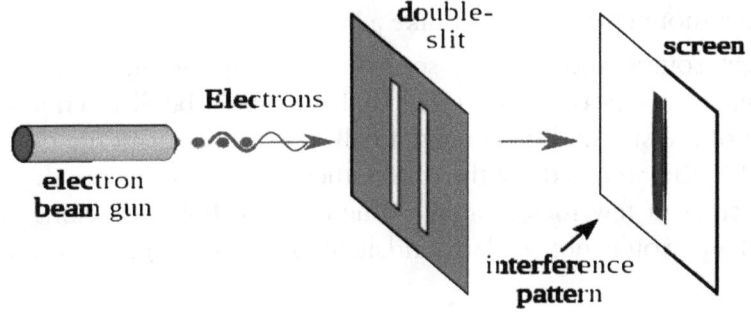

Young's Double Slit Experiment.[12]

Newton's theory of light was that it was made up of tiny particles, and they only ever moved in straight lines. Then, Huygens suggested that light was actually made up of waves and that these waves could bend, which meant they could affect and interfere with one another.

Back then, some scientists were more into Newton's idea than Huygens's. The way they saw it, Huygens's theory offered an obvious and far superior explanation for why light refracts and reflects than the wave theory. That didn't mean the corpuscular theory wasn't riddled with its own issues.

For instance, why can light diffract or bend around a slit or the edges of an object? Newton's theory could never explain that phenomenon. Why can light create colors when it comes in contact with thin films of oil slicks or soap bubbles? That was yet another question the corpuscular theory couldn't offer clarity on. It also didn't offer the best explanation for how light has the distinct trait of being unable to collide with each other whenever two or more beams are crossed with one another.

Young was taken with light and its nature. This physicist, also a physician, once saw light through the lens of the particle theory, but his investigations showed him the benefits of the wave theory, which did a good job of explaining the inexplicable. He found that light waves could actually interfere with each other.

"Interfere" in this context refers to the fact that light waves can cancel out and combine, depending on their relative positions. So, driven by his desire to learn all he could about light, he decided to do his famous Double-Slit Experiment.

Young kept it clean and classy. He didn't believe in complicating things for the sake of seeming impressive. The simplest way to replicate this experiment is to use an opaque object like a wall or a block, which has two slits carved in it. You would also need something to keep this object in place – and a monochromatic light (like a laser).

This light source should have something to support it, so the only reason it moves is *that you want it to*. The light should be directed toward the middle of the slits and positioned a half meter away from the double-slit object. On the other side of the object, there should be a smooth white wall or a screen a few meters away. When you've finished setting your experiment up, you'll notice dark and light bands showing up on your screen.

Laser light is excellent for this experiment because it can create a photon or more when it's powered with enough electricity, and those particles can emerge from the tiniest hole imaginable after a set period. Since the speed of light is not a variable but a fixed figure, it's possible to set a time for when the photons will appear on your screen.

If your laser's photons are created one after another, they'll appear as single light spots, proving they're particles. If they're waves, then it's natural to expect them to diverge or spread out as they push forward, and that means you'd expect to see a wide area of your screen being lit up – *but that's not what happens.* Photons being particles would imply that they should appear at two separate points on your screen or wall, but *that's not the case.*

Young didn't have access to lasers when he first carried out his experiment. He approached the process with the idea that light must be like water waves . . . and assumed that the light waves would travel from their source in the same way that ripples spread out when you drop a pebble in a lake. He also assumed that once the traveling wave hits the double slits, they'll become two distinct waves the moment they pass through the openings.

The light wouldn't show up as waves on the screen when Young did this experiment. Instead, it became obvious that the photons were hitting the screen on their own. Also, one of these particles could interfere with itself in the same way a wave would, according to classical physics. The photon could split once it got to the double-slit, only to reunite its parts once it hits the screen.

## The Photoelectric Effect (1887)

**Picture it:** A dark lab in Germany. The year is 1887. Heinrich Hertz, a 30-year-old, is hard at work, observing what happens when he shines an ultraviolet light beam onto a plate made of metal. He watches, fascinated, as the metal plate shoots off sparks. But it isn't really the emission that has his attention. You see, it's well known that metals are excellent electricity conductors since the electrons in this material aren't so rigidly connected to the atoms – meaning it won't take much to dislodge them with the right amount and intensity of energy.

So Hertz had a puzzle before him. He realized that the frequencies of the light bursts that made electron emission possible depended on the metal in question. He also noted that when he would turn up the light's brightness, there were more electrons emitted. Still, there wasn't a correlated increase in energy. When he used higher frequencies of light, he'd get electrons with increased energy. Still, there wasn't a commensurate increase in the number of electrons produced.

This phenomenon would eventually be dubbed the photoelectric effect, one which a young Albert Einstein would be able to fully explain later on in 1905. The photoelectric effect used to be quite a conundrum for classical physics, but it would also be one of the first wins Einstein scored during his career. This effect proves the fact that light is quantized.

**Here's a simpler breakdown of the effect.** When you shine a light on metal, electrons are emitted and then absorb the light. When these particles have enough energy, they'll set themselves free from the metal. Classical physics assumed light was only a wave and that there's no specific amount of energy that it swaps with the metal. The classical assumption, therefore, is that when you shine the light on the metallic object, the object's electrons absorb the light, and the energy gradually increases until there's enough to cause the electron emission process. Also, it was expected that when you shine even more light on the metal, you should notice the emitted particles move with a much higher kinetic energy. On the flip side, if the light is too weak, there's no way the metal can throw off electrons unless enough time passes.

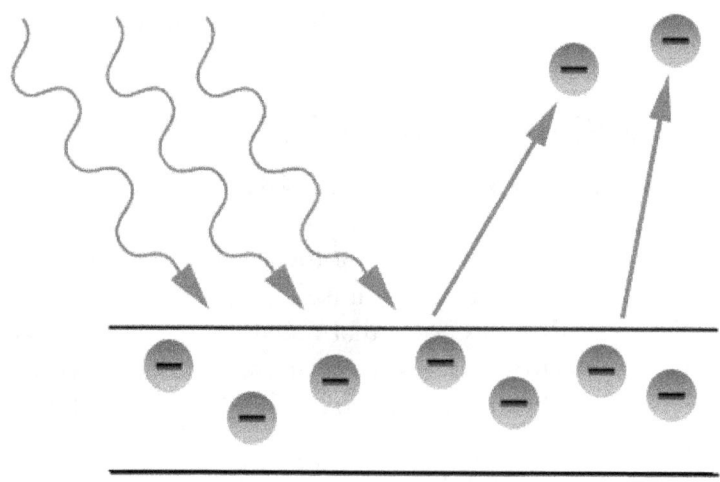

The Photoelectric Effect.[18]

Here's the thing: the experiment showed that these assumptions were false. The particles emitted the moment the light hit the metal, and regardless of how intensely bright or dim the light was, there would still be an immediate emission of electrons. So, the only thing you need to instigate that process is the frequency of the light rather than the intensity. Einstein would find an apt explanation inspired by Planck, and that's why he claimed light was quantized into photons, which meant it acted like waves and particles.

**So, what's really happening when light strikes the metal object?** The photons (light particles) collide with the loose electrons, and each electron swallows up each photon. When the photon has more energy than the object's work function, the electron is emitted. The formula that demonstrates this is written like this: $h\nu = W + K$, with W being the work function of the metal and K being the emitted electron's kinetic energy. To be clear, "work function" refers to the least amount of energy you would need to knock an electron free from a material. The material is usually metal.

## The Stern-Gerlach Experiment (1922)

What's the Stern-Gerlach experiment about? Well, it was the experiment that showed scientists that spin is a real thing – and no, not "spin" in the public-relations-Edward -Bernays type of way! To put a rather pedestrian spin on the definition of this concept, think of a spinning top. That's a rough analogy of how the tiny little particles that make up life move.

Otto Stern and Walther Gerlach were responsible for the revelation of this angular momentum. How did they discover it? Well, they had a beam of silver atoms channeled through magnetic poles, allowing it to hit a screen. What's interesting about this is the fact that silver has 47 electrons, but only 46 of them are arranged in a symmetrical cloud, which means they're not responsible for the atom's spin. What about the 47th electron? It's either in its 5s state or 5p state.

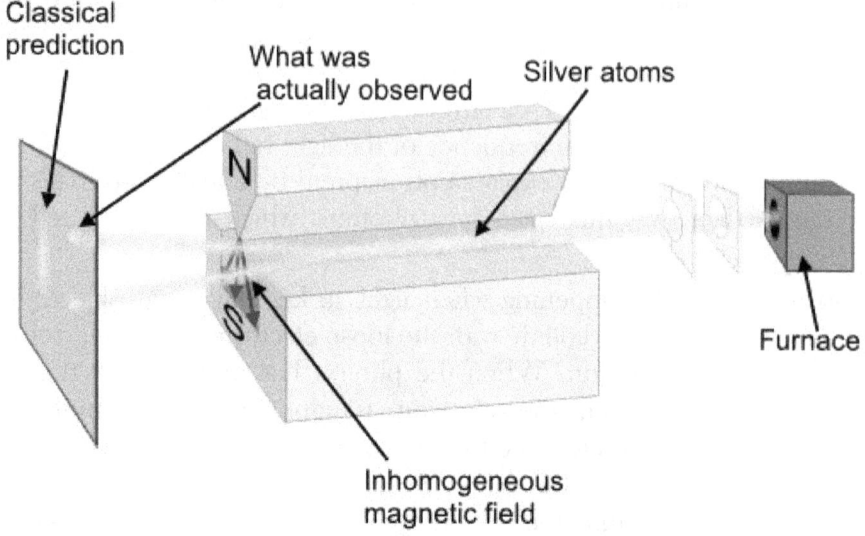

Theresa Knott[4]

An atom is not unlike a solar system but on a microcosmic level. In the middle of the atom is the nucleus, acting like the sun in the sky. As planets surround the sun, so do electrons surround the nucleus. Now, the electrons must travel through or occupy certain energy levels or lanes, which you can call "states." So, when silver's 47th electron is in the 5s state, there's no wobble or tilt as it travels a straight path while orbiting the nucleus, which means its angular momentum or spin has a value of 0.

Now, when this special electron is in the 5p state, its path is tilted as it travels around the nucleus, which means its angular momentum has a value of 1. The 5p state means the electron moves in one of three directions. If it's tilting down, the value of the spin is -1. When it's tilting up, it's +1. When there's no tilt, it's at 0. Are you confused about why the electron with no tilt is still in its 5p state rather than 5s? The 5p electron with no tilt may seem the same as the 5s, but it's actually on a different path.

Stern and Gerlach had thought they'd find one or three spots on the screen as they beamed their silver atoms through the magnet poles, but there were only two. Scientists would find this puzzling for a whopping three years, as they tried to find a theory to explain what was going on. The answer was discovered in 1925 by George E. Uhlenbeck and Samuel A. Goudsmit, whoh postulated that the electrons had intrinsic angular momentum.

Besides the angular momentum of the electrons, as they spin around the nucleus, they found there was an inner angular momentum or spin. The Stern-Gerlach experiment demonstrated that the beam of silver atoms splits in two, and this split depends on the way the 47th electron spins. Scientists learned that there are two kinds of spins, one up and the other down.

There's nothing in classical physics that talks about the idea of spin. It's only a quantum mechanical phenomenon. Even the analogy of the Earth spinning on its axis while spinning around the sun isn't the best one to explain spin. Also, if you could somehow stop an electron and put it in a state of inertia, it would still have its intrinsic spin. You can't take that away from it.

## The EPR Paradox (1935)

Also called the Einstein-Podolsky-Rosen Paradox, this is an interesting thought experiment that's meant to illustrate an intrinsic paradox that scientists tried to wrap their minds around when quantum theory was yet in its infancy. It's one of the best demonstrations of the concept of quantum entanglement. So what's it about?

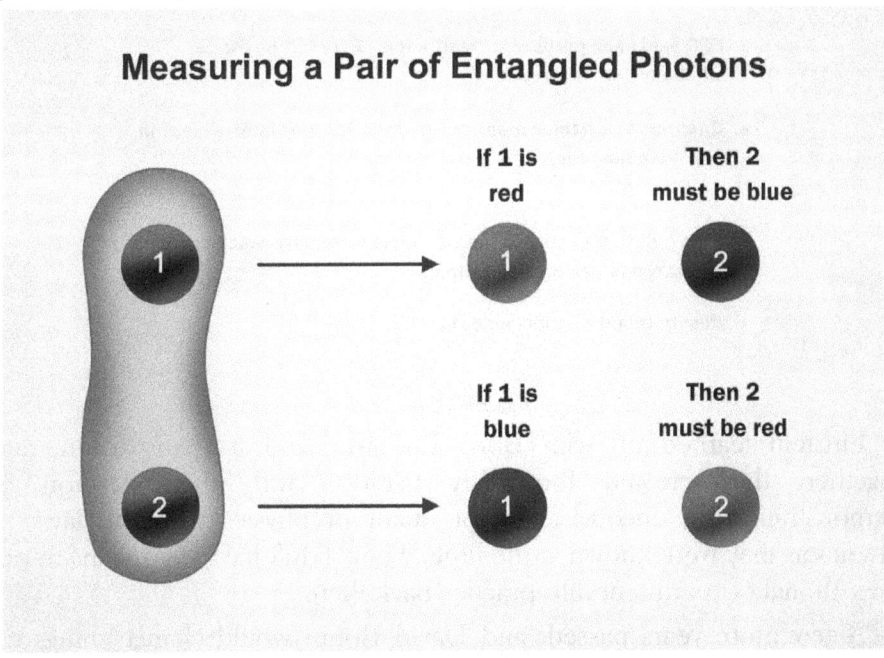

Measuring a pair of entangled photons.

Picture two particles entangled with each other. Until you measure each of them, they remain in a state of uncertainty. When you measure one, then it takes on a state of certainty, and so does the other yet unmeasured particle it's entangled with. As you've learned, this magic is possible because they both communicate with each other at speeds beyond the speed of light, which immediately calls into question Einstein's Relativity Theory.

This EPR Paradox was something Albert Einstein and Niels Bohr both exchanged intellectual blows over. You see, Einstein didn't want to accept quantum mechanics with open arms, while Bohr and his supporters were developing this field even further. What's interesting about this is Bohr's work was actually based on something Einstein had begun.

## EPR Paradox & Bell Inequality
### Einstein, Podolsky, Rosen experiment (Continued)

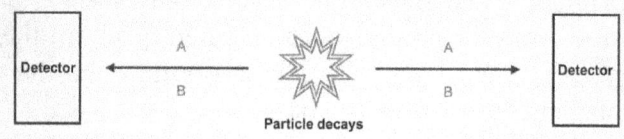

Particle decays

- EPR said each particle is "real" -- it is "A" or "B" no matter what any detector says.
- Quantum Mechanics predicts two particles are "intertwined" in one wave function.
  Neither particle is in a definite state (A or B) until it is detected.
- John Bell (1964) constructed a simple inequality which could be measured to decide who is right.
- Result: Quantum Mechanics is right.

**The EPR Paradox.**

Einstein teamed up with Boris Podolsky and Nathan Rosen, and together, they created the EPR Paradox with the intention of demonstrating the inconsistency of quantum physics with the laws of physics as they were known at the time. They didn't have the means to put their thought experiment into practice back then.

A few more years passed, and David Bohm would change things up with the EPR paradox example, with a view to making it easier to understand. Even the top physicists' unstable spin 0 (zero) decays of the time couldn't quite explain the paradox. In Bohm's version, a particle with an unstable spin 0 decays (or transforms) into two other particles, different from one another and moving in opposing directions, one clockwise and the other counterclockwise.

Since the original particle's spin was 0, the new particles have the same value in their spins. If one of them has spin +1/2, the other will have spin -1/2. Also, the Copenhagen interpretation of quantum mechanics holds that these particles don't have definite states until they're measured, as there's an equal chance they'll either have a negative or positive spin.

## Schrödinger's Cat (1935)

Now it's time to get to know Schrödinger's cat a little bit better. This was a thought experiment that scientists used to test out other quantum ideas, and it was born in the brilliant mind of Erwin Schrödinger, in 1935. He came up with this because of how quantum mechanics were explained according to the Copenhagen interpretation, which was that particles in the context of quantum mechanics are in existence in every state you can imagine simultaneously, *unless and until they are observed*, and only then do they select one out of the plethora of states to adhere to.

For instance, you could have a light bulb that, when lit, could either be red or green. When you're not looking at the light bulb, the Copenhagen interpretation of quantum mechanics would have you assume that the light the bulb emits is both colors, red and green. Yet, when you do look at the light, it will have to be one or the other, not both. This wasn't something Schrödinger agreed with, and this was why he'd introduce the world to his cat experiment.

Here's the thought experiment in a nutshell. Pretend, for a moment, that you have a cat. Not only that, but you also have a small piece of some radioactive substance, which is something that's unstable and emits particles randomly. Now, you place both your cat and this radioactive object into a box and seal it in.

Also, you rig the box with a device that will release poison into it. This is no ordinary poison. It can only kill the cat if the device picks up on one of the particles emitted by the radioactive substance. Once the radioactive substance decays, it emits particles, triggering the device (a Geiger counter) to go off. Once triggered, the device releases poison that leads to the totally unjust and horrendous death of your cat.

When you consider the observation theory and bring it to bear in this experiment, since no one's watching the cat (remember it's sealed in a box, and you don't have x-ray vision), the cat has to be both dead and alive. Why? The radioactive substance will decay and won't decay. The poison will and won't be released. At least, not until you open up the box to check on your cat, at which point it will then be one or the other. Looking in on your cat is the same as "measuring" the outcome, which is the process thought to force the cat to either be okay or give up one of its nine lives. Schrödinger's point was that this was an absurd thought and an impossibility in real life for the cat to be in both states. He demonstrated with this thought experiment that the cause of wave-function collapse has nothing to do with whether there's an observer or not.

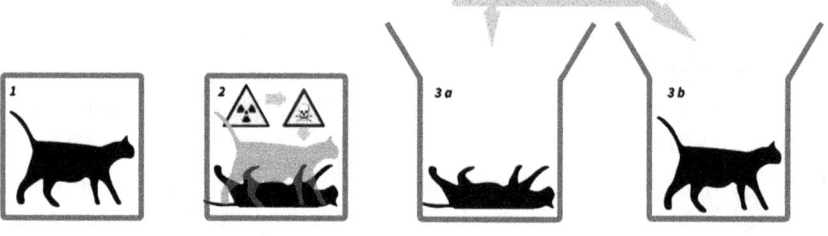

Schrödinger's cat experiment.[15]

As Nobel Prize winner and physicist Robert Penrose would later write in his book *The Road to Reality*, the cat being both dead and alive simultaneously is absurd when looked at in the context of the physical world. He pointed out there's a 50-50 chance of the cat being dead or alive, strictly physically speaking, and that this is proof of the fault in all interpretations of Schrödinger's cat that seek to prove the cat is in both states at the same time. Schrödinger demonstrated how impossible it is for things to exist in a state of superposition in real life. Unless, of course, there's more to life than meets the eye.

## The Delayed Choice Quantum Eraser (1998)

Early in 1998, Yoon-Ho Kim, R. Yu, S. P. Kulik, Y. H. Shih, and Marlan O. Scully worked on the Delayed Choice Quantum Eraser experiment.

The point of this experiment was to probe further into the results of the double-slit experiment, as well as where quantum entanglement ultimately leads.

The scientists worked with a Spontaneous Parametric Down-Conversion laser beam and a Beta-Barium Borate crystal (also called a BBO crystal). The laser beam they chose was a powerful one, which, when directed onto the right crystal, will cause the light to split into pairs of much weaker photons than contained in the original beam.

The photons being shot out of the SPDC laser beam and onto the BBO crystal are in pairs. They are entangled, so whatever you observe by studying one of the pair of particles is definitely happening to its twin, regardless of their distance from each other. When the photons are shot at the double-slit wall, each photon in a pair could choose to pass through one slit or the other.

Beyond the slits, there's a device that detects which slit every particle or photon passes through. Still, the catch is you can turn it on or off only after the photons have passed through these slits – and this is where the fun begins. When you check to see which slit the photons chose to pass through, you'll notice they have particle-like traits because they'll either pass through one slit or the other, but never will they go through both.

What about when you don't track the paths of the particles with the device? In that case, the photons become like waves, which means they pass through both slits simultaneously and create a rippling pattern. The even weirder thing is whatever you decide seems to determine how the photons *acted in the past.* You might as well call these photons psychic because it's like they knew if you'd use the device to track their path or not. This is why it's called "delayed choice." The "eraser" bit suggests that one outcome or nature of the photons is erased in favor of the other.

What's really going on with these psychic particles? Well, they're not exactly psychic, nor do they have the ability to go back in time and change things. What this experiment does is present a challenge to the way everyone has always assumed time works. The classical idea of time is linear. In other words, your present is supposed to be the sum total of your past, and your present determines your future.

This experiment suggests time may not be linear and that all three faces of time are intertwined with one another in ways that continue to baffle scientists even now. As fascinating as all this is, some insist that the retrocausality suggested by the experiment is misunderstood.

# Interpretations of Quantum Mechanics

There are various ways to interpret quantum mechanics and its theories. Here's a quick look at some of them.

**The Copenhagen Interpretation:** Of the many interpretations out there, this is the most accepted one, founded on the idea that particles act in line with the probability wave notion – and that superposition is valid. According to this interpretation, the act of observation of measurement forces wave function to select or collapse to one state only (probability wave), and particles can be in more than one place at the same time (superposition).

**The Many-Worlds Interpretation:** The idea behind this interpretation is that there isn't a fixed history or future and that multiple versions exist because there's more than one universe or world. So, in the quantum world, the universe splits into several more with each event that occurs.

**The Pilot-Wave Theory:** The distinguishing feature of this interpretation is that there are hidden variables in the quantum world, and this is why all the random, unpredictable, spooky action in quantum mechanics happens. This is also called the *De Broglie-Bohm Theory*.

**Quantum Bayesianism:** Also known as *QBism*, the interpretation suggests your beliefs about a system's state are what play out as the wave function.

**Objective Collapse Theories:** These interpretations have the premise that the wave function collapse isn't relegated to the quantum world but is physical and real.

**Relational Quantum Mechanics:** Through this lens of interpretation, you assume that the same series of events may be observed and interpreted differently depending on the context.

**Transactional Interpretation:** The wave nature of the particles in the quantum world matters when viewing quantum affairs through this context, and waves and particles are equally important as they complement each other.

What's the point of all these interpretations? They're all attempts by philosophers and physicians to describe the *true nature of reality*. Where one interpretation falls short, another may pick up the slack and offer explanations that make sense.

# Chapter 5: Quantum Reality and Consciousness

You can't learn about quantum physics without beginning to question the nature of reality. Quantum reality and consciousness remain matters of intense debate, drawing scientific and non-scientific minds alike. In this chapter, you'll open your mind to the thought that consciousness has a deeper role in life as you know it than you could ever imagine.

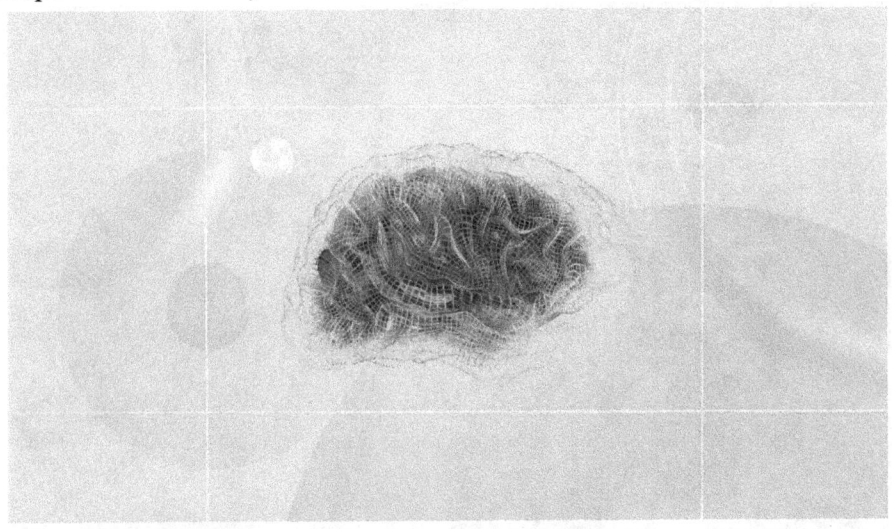

Quantum reality and consciousness remain matters of intense debate.[16]

# Quantum Mind Theories

Quantum mind theories attempt to explain consciousness as clearly as possible so that humanity understands itself better. Think of how your mind works. Do you assume it's all just neurons doing their thing in your brain? Well, quantum mind theories suggest there's more at play. The inner workings of your mind depend on quantum rules, and this is what makes human consciousness so dynamic, rich, and fascinating.

Quantum mind, also called quantum consciousness, is a set of theories or hypotheses that put forth the idea that superposition, entanglement, and other quantum physics events are what create consciousness. Consciousness, a subjective and personal thing, is a tough nut to crack using quantum physics, but there have been a few interesting quantum mind theories put forth that seem to explain it.

David Chalmers is the philosopher who coined the term "the hard problem of consciousness." What is this problem? Well, how do the physical actions of your brain cells cause your subjective experience of life, if they even do? Why do you feel something as one thing rather than as another? What's responsible for your inner experience of life, which is different from others' inner experiences? Why do you even have an inner life in the first place?

David Chalmers coined the term "The hard problem of consciousness."[17]

The "hard problem of consciousness" is working out how and why living beings have subjective, conscious experiences, also called *"qualia."* It's one thing to know how and why certain aspects of the human brain make it possible to tell things apart from each other, to process and understand information, and to carry out specific actions. The explanations for those things are rooted in functionality and behaviorism, but the same doesn't apply to the hard problem of consciousness. Here's a look at some of the quantum mind theories that have been put forth to solve this hard problem.

## Bohm's Implicate Order

You know matter is whatever has weight and occupies space. As for consciousness, it's the ability you have to be aware of yourself, others, and the world around you. It's being able to feel, perceive, and think. *Bohm's Implicate Order* is an attempt to find the thread that ties consciousness, matter, and quantum physics.

According to Bohm, there's more to reality than meets the eye. There's a deeper level where everything is connected to everything else, thanks to quantum phenomena. Bohm referred to this deep level as the Implicate Order – to reflect the fact that this level is hidden from regular observation. Being a creative person, he had another term for the Implicate Order: the *Holomovement*, which describes a movement that's complete or whole.

To conceptualize the Implicate order, think of it as an ocean that stretches as far as the eyes can see. You notice that this ocean is full of waves, and each of those waves represents a possibility in the quantum field. Bohm believed that the waves could overlap with each other, and this interference creates intricate patterns that you pick up on as consciousness and matter in the reality he called the Explicate Order (the visible, individual ocean waves with no overlap).

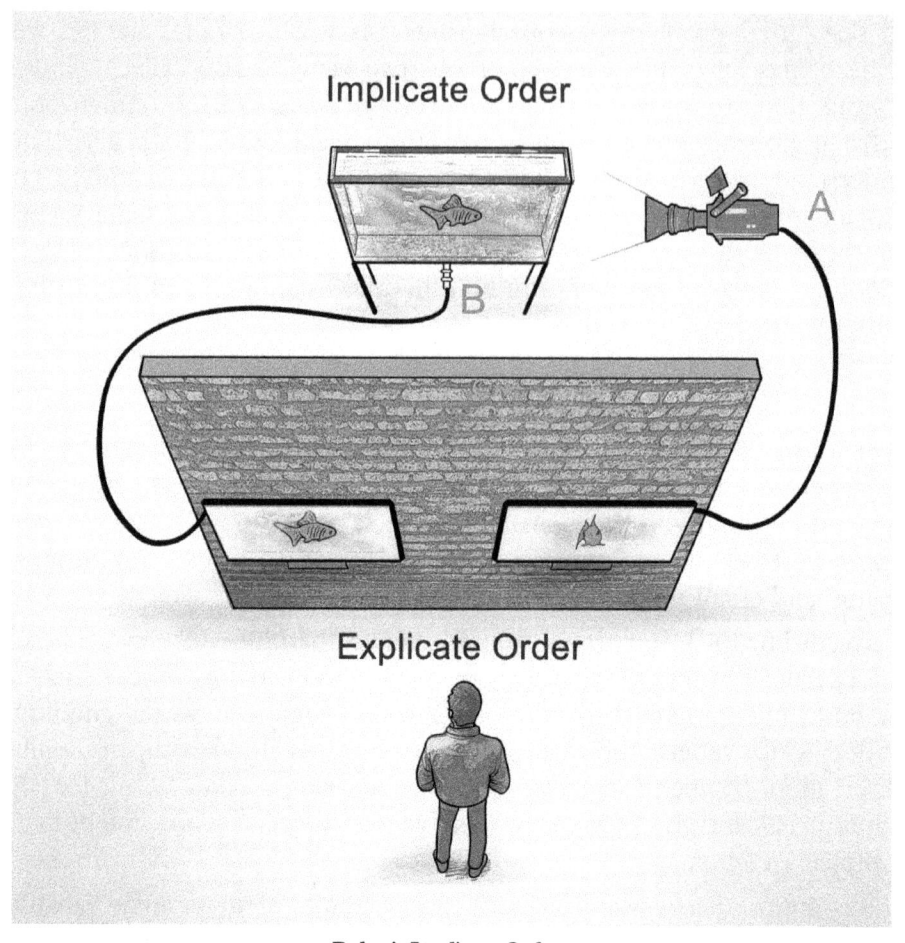

**Bohm's Implicate Order.**

Bohm says that matter and consciousness aren't to be seen as separate phenomena but as sharing the same foundational reality while presenting differing aspects. In other words, they're both born from the Implicate Order and reflect it. Consciousness, therefore, is the Implicate Order reflecting itself to itself, while matter is the manifestation of the Implicate Order in space and time.

The Implicate Order is ever in motion and always creative. It's in the business of crafting new forms and making room for new possibilities. The analogy Bohm drew was that of a hologram, which, if you haven't seen one in the movies, is a 3D image generated by lasers. When you break a hologram up into bits, you'll discover perfectly whole versions of the original hologram in each piece.

The same thing is happening with every part of the Implicate Order and the Explicit Order. In other words, whether it's the entire ocean or a drop of ocean water, they're both the same ocean with the same components. This isn't an easy thing for mainstream physicists to accept, and they keep coming up against challenge after challenge, trying to prove or even test this quantum mind theory.

## Penrose-Hameroff Orchestrated Objective Reduction (Orch-OR)

According to Roger Penrose and Stuart Hameroff, the founders of the Orchestrated Objective Reduction (Orch-OR) theory, it makes no sense to assume that the neural networks in your brain are the only things responsible for your consciousness. They hold that there's some quantum computation going on as well.

Penrose and Hameroff say microtubules contain the quantum processes on which your brain works. Microtubules are small protein tubes within your neurons or brain cells, responsible for cell division, movement, and communication. These microtubules are also responsible for giving your neurons their structure. It isn't your brain cells generating consciousness but the events occurring at a quantum level *within* the cells.

Think of these microcomputers as quantum computers that process information on that microscopic level. The fact that they can create quantum superpositions implies these "computers" can be in a variety of states at the same time until the observer effect kicks in. They're so amazing they also create quantum entanglements, allowing them to connect with one another and create changes across space.

The thing about these states is they switch up their functions depending on the environment. They're subject to decoherence, where they collapse into one state. This is the very reason quantum computers have to run in environments with low temperatures and far from all disturbances.

Penrose and Hameroff claim your brain can avoid the decoherence effect, holding on to the coherence within its microtubules for an impressive period. With your memory, senses, and bureau structures, you can dictate the processes going on in your microtubules at the quantum level. But the question is, what connection do the quantum neural processes have with consciousness? How do they create it? Enter objective reduction (OR).

OR is a version of quantum collapse thanks to spacetime's nature rather than the observer effect or decoherence. What's space-time? It's the tapestry of the universe, the combination of space and time, that creates a fourth-dimension spectrum or continuum.

Once the microtubules are super-positioned, and things hit a level of instability, that's OR. Superposition is forced to collapse into one state, and this process is the birth of consciousness. The collapse, fortunately, doesn't need any observer to occur, as it happens on its own. Also, once it happens, you can't undo it or reverse it. Would you like to try to compute which choice it will make? You can't. There's not one algorithm that exists that could predict what's going on, and you could say this is the explanation of concepts such as creativity and free will.

Why did Penrose and Hameroff refer to this as orchestrated objective reduction? The way they saw it, your brain is what determines the location in space and the point in time of these OR occurrences in the microtubules, which leads to conscious moment after conscious moment, or what you'd call a "stream of consciousness." These scientists also held that the Platonic values are rooted in the framework of spacetime, which includes ethical values, mathematical truth, and aesthetic beauty.

## The Quantum Zeno Effect

Another name for this effect is the Turing Paradox. This effect is about the fact that particles and other quantum systems could be forced to collapse into a specific state or "frozen" by measuring it as frequently as required, which keeps it from being superpositioned.

Remember, at the quantum level of existence, superposition is the order of the day because all particles are in all states at the same time until there's a wave-function collapse forcing it into a specific, unchanging state. According to the Quantum Zeno Effect, when you keep your eye on a particle long enough, you force it to remain in its original state. It loses its ability to change.

Here is a simplification of the effect in action. You're on YouTube. In your mind, the white line that indicates how much of the video has loaded is in a race against the red line, which shows how much of the video you've watched so far.

Unfortunately, the red line has caught up with the white one, and now, thanks to your internet working at the neck-breaking speed of a snail, you're forced to wait for the video to load so you can resume watching.

You get sick and tired of waiting for the white line to load some more already. You're eyeing it like a hawk.

According to the Quantum Zeno Effect, the fact that you keep checking on the video's loading progress is the real reason it's not loading. It's like with the proverbial watched kettle that never boils; the only thing boiling is your impatience. Thankfully, your internet service provider can't use this as an excuse for why your videos get stuck buffering at the good bits.

What's with "Zeno" in the name of this effect? Have you ever heard of Zeno's arrow paradox? This is a puzzle of sorts, dating all the way back to ancient Greece. According to Zeno, the Greek philosopher of Elea, when you look at an arrow in flight at any point in time, it appears not to be moving. His argument, therefore, was that the flying arrow isn't actually moving.

Time is a series of moments or instances, and there's no motion in each moment or motion. Therefore, the arrow is still. It's the same thing with the Quantum Zeno Effect, as it appears that quantum systems operate the same way by freezing upon constant measurement or observation.

Now, what connection does the Quantum Zeno Effect have with consciousness? The idea is that all consciousness is affected by this effect, and by consciously observing these processes, you can influence them, freezing them into a state and thereby keeping them from changing.

For instance, if your consciousness is the result of the quantum superpositions in your brain, and you were to somehow monitor these superpositions consciously, that would keep the super-positioned processes from changing, which could be a viable explanation for how physical processes generate consciousness in the first place.

## Consciousness, Spirituality, and Psychology

Being conscious is being aware. It's knowing you exist in space and time. Consciousness is the stuff that makes you feel like a real person, alive and kicking, different from the people and other creatures around you. Yet, as clear and obvious as it seems, certain aspects of consciousness can be rather difficult to pin down. It isn't yet fully understood how the brain and its neural processes can create consciousness, nor how consciousness is tied to your perception of the physical world. Some suggest that consciousness is not a product of the brain but that the brain itself and everything else in the observable world is the creation of consciousness.

People like the Dalai Lama see a connection between consciousness, spirituality, and quantum physics. The way he sees it, every atom in your body is an inextricable part of everything that makes up the world. You're literally made of star stuff. Your body has carbon, nitrogen, and oxygen, elements that were forged in fiery stars over 4.5 billion years ago. You're also intrinsically connected to every other thing on Earth, as you're made of energy like everything else on Earth.

**People like the Dalai Lama see a connection between consciousness, spirituality, and quantum physics.[18]**

You know how difficult it is for spiritualists and scientists to see eye to eye. If you could travel back in time through some awesome quantum process to the Middle Ages and even the Renaissance, you'd witness this war between head and heart in real-time. Back then, any scientific progress was deemed dangerous, demonized, and was enough cause for murder.

Over time, the pendulum has swung to the other extreme, with spirituality being mocked by the world of science. So, how fascinating is it that, finally, there may be one thing where experts in both fields see eye to eye, especially when it comes to quantum physics and Buddhist philosophy?

Quantum physics demonstrates there's a world beyond the physical, one made of energy. Buddhists also agree with this, as their religion makes it clear that the physical must be transcended to give your full attention to your consciousness, which is what gives life its form and meaning in the first place.

This lends further credence to the quote by the late, great 17th-century French philosopher René Descartes: *"Cogito, ergo sum,"* meaning, "I think, therefore I am." It's your thoughts and your consciousness that shape your experience of life. This is also the foundation of many psychological practices, which seek to alter the mind's assumptions about life to help patients live as the versions of themselves they'd prefer to be.

The idea of consciousness being the true sculptor of life isn't something only Buddhists know. For instance, Amit Goswami of the University of Oregon also backs up the idea that micro-particles will change the way they act *depending on your actions as the observer.* This is a point that has already been clearly explained in this book.

Scientists and spiritualists have put down their blowtorches and pitchforks to agree, for once, that you and the world around you are defined by your thoughts and emotions.

This proposition is a challenging one for those whose minds aren't flexible and who prefer to follow orthodox ways. The implication of all this could be summed up by this wonderful quote by R. C. Henry in *The Mental Universe*: *"If we think about the possible connection between quantum physics and spirituality, we can see that the mind would no longer be that accidental intruder in the realm of matter, but would rather rise as a creator and governing entity of the realm of matter."*

## Observation

Each time you interact with the quantum system, you are observing or measuring it. By using a macroscopic device such as a detector to look at an atom or a photon, you cause the wave function collapse that moves the atom or other particle from a state where it's everywhere and everything at once into a single form and location.

The act of observing the particle moves it from the realm of the indefinite to the definite. While you may understand this theoretically, it remains one of the most perplexing things that quantum physicists struggle to grasp.

It is one thing to understand the observer effect, but it's another thing entirely to know why it happens. What is it about someone being consciously aware of an atom that forces it to crystallize into a specific state? What even counts as an observer? Does it have to be someone with consciousness, like a human being, or could it be a device monitoring the particles on its own with no interference?

If you look at this phenomenon through the lens of the Copenhagen interpretation, the von Neumann-Wigner interpretation, as well as the many-minds interpretation, they all agree on one thing: An observer's consciousness is the key to forcing a wave function collapse to happen. You would be forgiven for assuming they're basically saying you have superpowers.

Other interpretations of this phenomenon do not suggest that the observer's consciousness has any relevance in causing the collapse of the wave function. According to these theories, collapse is something that happens objectively. When that's not the case, then it must be an illusion of sorts, which is a result of the particles interacting with their environment.

If you choose to view the collapse of wave function through this particular school of thought, then you have to stay away from the problems and paradoxes that come up as a result of introducing the element of consciousness. In other words, you would have no business with Schrodinger's cat.

It's not a new thing to suggest that consciousness plays a huge part in the crafting of physical reality. In addition to Buddhism, Taoism and Hinduism also have their own takes on this process. They suggest that the world as you observe it is an illusion, also known as *Maya*. According to these religions, there lies a "true" and "real" reality, so to speak, beneath the physical world, which is consciousness itself.

Those who follow these spiritual paths refer to this consciousness as Brahman, the Buddha nature, or the Tao. Reading their religious texts, it becomes clear that intention and thought are the only ways to influence the physical world. So, when you combine that idea with the observer effect, it becomes clear that whatever you observe is a result of your thoughts, emotions, and expectations.

Moving away from traditional Eastern philosophies and onto esotericism, mysticism, and occultism, the claim is that the physical world is a creation of the spiritual one. These forms of spirituality also agree that the way to alter your physical life is by using the power of intention and thought.

Other modalities to achieve this influence include meditation, prayer, visualization, magic, rituals, etc. These practices are meant to assist you in harnessing consciousness and molding it to achieve whatever goals you desire. This is also the logic behind how the impossible is accomplished, such as healing terminal diseases, receiving divine protection and timely provision, or inexplicable transformations.

## Consciousness and the Quantum Field

You've become best buds with Schrödinger's cat. It's time to meet someone new: Wigner's friend.

Who's that?

Well, it's more like, *what's* that? It is a thought experiment that's a twist on Schrödinger's cat. Before you get acquainted, you should know that consciousness isn't an individual thing.

Every thought and sensation you've ever had or will ever have, every image you've conjured or come across, and every feeling you've experienced all spring from consciousness. These things also return to consciousness in the same way subatomic particles behave when it comes to the quantum field.

Now, back to the cat. It's in a sealed box, and its life depends on whether or not a radioactive atom expels poison that kills it. Remember, this cat is alive *and* dead as long as the box stays sealed. Wigner's friend comes over to observe this experiment. They have no idea whether the cat is alive or dead. When Wigner's friend opens the box and looks at the cat, that very act forces the wave function to collapse, and this means the cat is either dead or, better yet, alive.

Wigner's friend forces one and all to question what role consciousness may have had in the cat's fate, if any. In other words, is it possible that your mind is so powerful it affects events on a quantum level? This thought experiment clearly demonstrates the interplay between consciousness and the quantum world. You could say your new friend validates the observer effect, double-slit experiment, delayed-choice quantum eraser, and quantum Zeno effect.

The connection between the quantum field and consciousness is something that physicists continue to explore. For instance, Dr. Dirk K. F. Meiher, a professor at the University of Groningen in the Netherlands, thinks of consciousness as being within a field that's found around your brain, residing in a different dimension. He proposes that your brain pulls information from this field as needed through the quantum mechanism of entanglement and other quantum activities.

Not only that, but Meiher also believes the field is no different than a black hole in certain ways and is able to draw information from dark energy, Earth's magnetic field, and other interesting sources. You could call this field a meta-cognitive domain or a global memory space, very much like how the digital cloud saves all sorts of information on your behalf, ready for you to retrieve what you need when you need it.

The implications of Meiher's suggestions are significant because if consciousness isn't something your brain generates, and if there's a larger field from which it comes, that could only mean humanity must begin to question the material way it views the world.

You have to wonder about whether or not you have free will, what this implies about your identity, and what is really real. That said, you should now see the importance of self-awareness. It doesn't hurt to know what you're putting out with your thoughts and emotions since these will automatically draw corresponding experiences and other effects from the quantum field into your life, for better or worse.

## Self-Awareness Exercises

If you want to become more self-aware, then look no further than practicing mindfulness meditation. Sure, it's a great tool to help you bust stress and stay healthy, but it does a whole lot more than that for you. You will experience a profound connection with the present, moving from moment to moment with full awareness rather than remaining stuck in past regrets or future worries. Perform the following exercises each day for phenomenal results.

### Body Scan

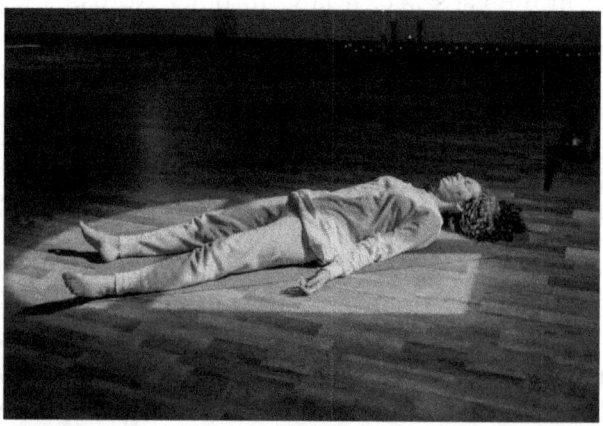

The body scan meditation is a great way to tap into your self-awareness.[19]

1. Lie or sit comfortably. This should be a position you can hold for at least ten to fifteen minutes without needing to adjust your body.
2. Close your eyes and bring your attention to your breathing. Notice the pattern of your breath without trying to control it.
3. Now, begin breathing deeply, allowing tensions to seep out of your body with each exhale.
4. When you feel more relaxed than you did at the start of this exercise, bring your attention to your feet. Scan every part of each part of them. How do your feet feel? Are you picking up on any sensations? Is there tension? Take a deep breath in, imagining you're breathing light into your feet, and then exhale slowly, releasing all tension and discomfort from them as you do.
5. Move your attention up to your calves and do the same thing you did in step 4. Work your way up your whole body, front and back, until you arrive at the crown of your head. Remember, breathe out the tension in each part.

**Deliberate Acceptance**
1. Sit somewhere silent, free from devices, distractions, and disturbances.
2. Take a few deep breaths and become aware of the present moment.
3. Now, pay attention to the thoughts and feelings that well up within you.
4. As each thought or feeling floats into your conscious awareness, accept it. Regardless of how boring or bizarre it is, don't attempt to fight or judge it. See them for what they are: fluctuations in your mental field.
5. As you observe your feelings and thoughts, notice how they bob up to the surface of your awareness and dissolve while you remain detached from them. Understand that this process is how you place yourself in a state where you observe quantum probabilities.

Do you get the feeling that this book suddenly took quite a sharp turn? That's deliberate. You have a rudimentary understanding of quantum physics. Now, it's time to take what you've learned so far and see how it all fits in with the mystical, spiritual aspects of life. You're on the train to the Twilight Zone. Buckle up and remain safely seated with your hands, arms, feet, and legs in the vehicle at all times.

# Chapter 6: Quantum Mysticism – Science and Spirituality

The connection between quantum mechanics and spirituality may not be immediately obvious, kind of like how you'd never think of mixing ice cream with a bowl of chicken noodle soup!

When it comes to all things quantum, there's a connection between science and spirit, as you'll soon discover in this chapter. The interplay between both fields will offer you some of the most intriguing ways to view reality, your identity, and your role in the grand scheme of life and the universe.

Before the ride begins, know that quantum mysticism isn't something accepted by the entire scientific community. Some say it's an oversimplification of the

When it comes to all things quantum, there's a connection between science and spirit.[20]

intricate nature of quantum mechanics at best or a misrepresentation of quantum principles at worst. Nevertheless, quantum mysticism will make you think long and hard and give you some *aha* moments about the weird things you've noticed about your life.

## The Ride Begins: Key Aspects of Quantum Mysticism

Some people call quantum mysticism "quantum woo" or "quantum quackery" because they think it's ridiculous. If they took a moment, they'd find their derision is rooted in fear because they're scared of the implications that science and spirituality can find common ground, and they'd be forced to reevaluate their preconceived notions about life and how it works.

Thankfully, Deepak Chopra, Stuart Hameroff, Fritjof Capra, Gary Zukav, Lawrence LeShan, Arthur Koestler, the Fundamental Fysiks Group, and other great minds in the New Age space are unperturbed by pejorative opinions on quantum mysticism and have played their part in bringing it to the forefront of humanity's awareness. They couldn't care less either about Wikipedia's obvious push to make it seem like nothing more than "woo woo" nonsense. Quantum mysticism is the metaphysical bridge that connects quantum physics to consciousness, mysticism, and spirituality. What are the key aspects and ideas of this field?

**Non-Locality:** According to classical physics, locality is a principle that suggests the only way there could be any physical interaction between two particles or objects is when they're near each other. In other words, the further apart they are, the less likely they are to affect one another.

Quantum physics suggests this classical take on locality leaves much to be desired in explaining spooky action at a distance. It suggests non-locality instead, the idea that it doesn't matter how far apart particles are once they're entangled. They'll always affect one another, regardless of how many galaxies or lightyears you put between them.

Looking at non-locality through the lens of quantum mysticism, it's apparent that everything in the world is intricately connected. If everything is really made up of subatomic systems, whether photons, electrons, quarks, or other particles, there's something that keeps it all connected.

You're connected to the entire cosmos. In fact, you could say you *are* the cosmos. You're part of one great, big, cosmic soup of particles, all connected to one another. Electromagnetism, gravity, and quantum forces all work to connect all galaxies, planets, people, plants, animals, and objects to one another. So, whatever affects the one affects the whole - regardless of how much space or time is between them.

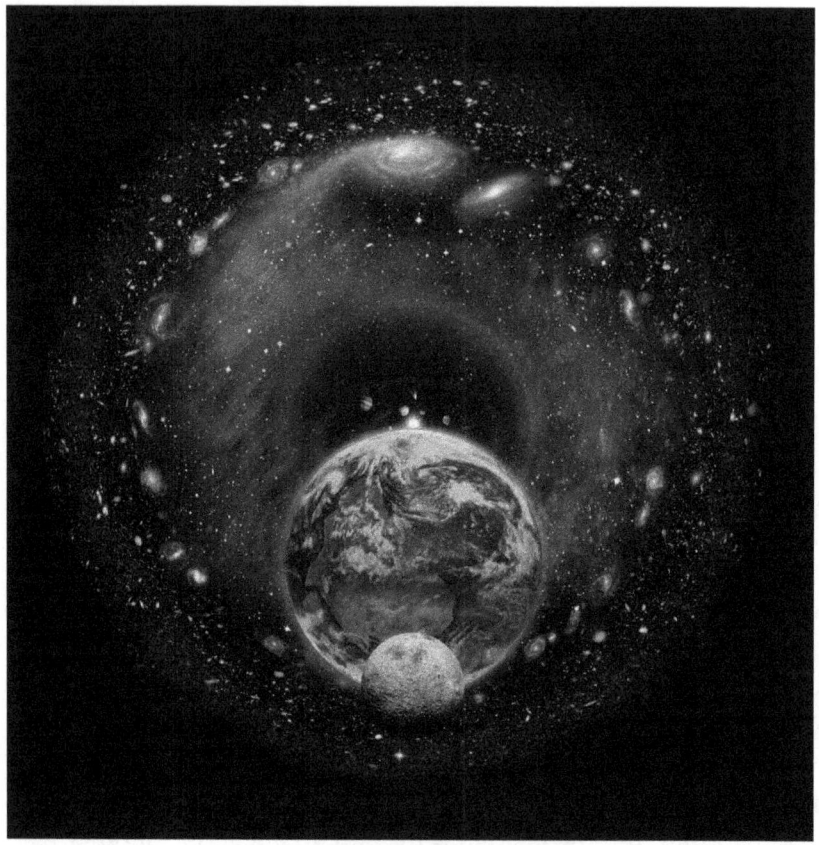

Quantum forces all work to connect all galaxies, planets, people, plants, animals, and objects to one another.[21]

**Interconnectedness and Unity:** You already understand the basic quantum premises of quantum physics that suggest all things are connected to one another, such as quantum entanglement. So, what's the connection to quantum mysticism? The Hermetic principle "As above, so below" captures this beautifully well, suggesting that the microcosm and the macrocosm reflect one another.

You are a reflection of the universe, and vice versa. The sacred texts of the Upanishads have the phrase "Tat Tvam Asi," which means "You are That." It essentially is about the fact that everything in existence is one and the same, an expression of divinity.

Buddhism has the idea of pratītyasamutpāda or paṭiccasmuppāda, which implies that all things are caused by something else. Put all of this together, and it's obvious to see how your thoughts, intentions, and emotions affect the world around you – and then some.

**Unity of Mind and Matter:** The observer effect clearly demonstrates that the observation process affects how reality plays out. Without a doubt, consciousness affects all quantum processes, which affect everything in all worlds, known and unknown.

Buddhists are well aware of this, as they believe in Sunyata, which means "emptiness." What's that about? Every phenomenon is connected to others. This idea is also called dependent origination, where nothing has an intrinsic nature.

Therefore, your life is defined by the phenomena surrounding you, which means your experiences, in turn, are determined by you. What makes a table a table, as opposed to a python? It is the fact that the table depends on other "surrounding" traits that define it as such. Who you are as a person depends on the environment or context you're in.

Your life isn't a permanently defined thing. A scammer could be someone else when they find themselves in a different context. "Context" isn't only the physical environment, but the mental as well. If there's something you don't like about your life or experience, changing your mental context or the way you view yourself is an excellent way to transform yourself into the person you would rather be.

**Reality Creation and Manifestation:** Put together all the previous key aspects of quantum mysticism, and it becomes obvious that you now have the keys to crafting the life of your dreams. While your life may appear firmly fixed and unchangeable, every particle remains in a state of superposition until you observe it.

Feeling stuck? It's time to take your attention off things as they are. You can do this by practicing mindfulness meditation, as you've learned in the previous chapter, remaining in a state of non-reactive awareness. You know there are infinite versions of you, including the one you desire.

So, from the non-reactive state, you turn your attention to a vision of yourself as you'd like to be. If you're not great at visualizing (another way to say "imagining pictures"), you could focus on the *feeling* you'd have as the person you desire to be. This is how you cause the wave function to collapse into this new, preferred version of reality. You live your life by observing yourself as this new person, thinking, feeling, and acting through them.

Thanks to quantum entanglement, the changes you've put in place in your mind will cause the world around you to adjust as needed, becoming more and more in alignment with the version of yourself you've "collapsed" into. Working with the quantum Zeno effect, you maintain your attention on being this preferred version of yourself, and this sustained attention or observation keeps you in this new reality you've chosen for yourself. This is how the Law of Attraction works.

## Unified Field Theory

Have you ever played with Lego blocks? If you have, you know they come in various colors, shapes, and sizes. Yet, despite their differences, they all connect together because they're designed to. The unified field theory, a term coined by Albert Einstein, is an attempt to connect all forces of physics to one another. It's about seeking the one theory to rule them all.

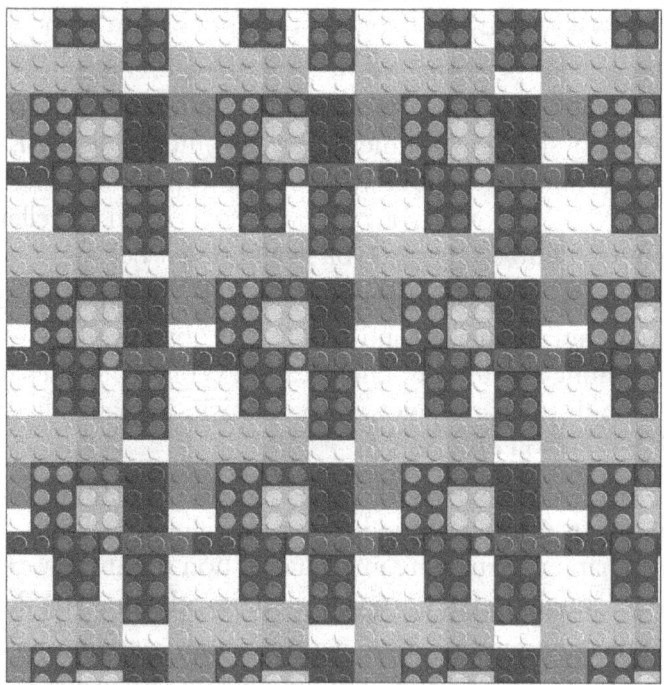

Legos are a good metaphor for how they connect together despite their differences.[22]

Physics dictates that it's not that these forces are transmitted from one particle or object to another. Rather, there are unique entities known as fields that are responsible for deploying these forces.

The unified field is a field that rules over every aspect of life, connecting the strong nuclear force, weak nuclear force, gravity, and electromagnetism. What this theory implies is that everything is connected at a fundamental level, and if there were a way to flesh out this theory accurately, the implications for physics and the breakthroughs to come would be beyond imagination.

Now, what about the quantum field? This field is what lies at the heart of all physical aspects of reality, containing information and energy in the form of virtual particles with the unique trait of being able to pop in and out of existence. If you want to understand why matter and energy are the way they are, look no further than the quantum field.

The unified field theory has the goal of uniting all of nature's forces, while the quantum field is the glue that holds all energies and particles together, whether you're thinking about subatomic particles or every single universe in existence. This field is responsible for the non-locality that connects one thing to all else.

Quantum mysticism explores the quantum field and unified field through spiritual lenses. Avid meditators in the zero thought or zero point state are simply connecting with these fields, from which they can craft the realities they prefer. The same applies to other mindfulness and spiritual practices, such as yoga. By making a habit of connecting with these fields each day, you'll experience a deep sense of appreciation for life, purpose, passion, joy, and oneness with everyone and everything around you.

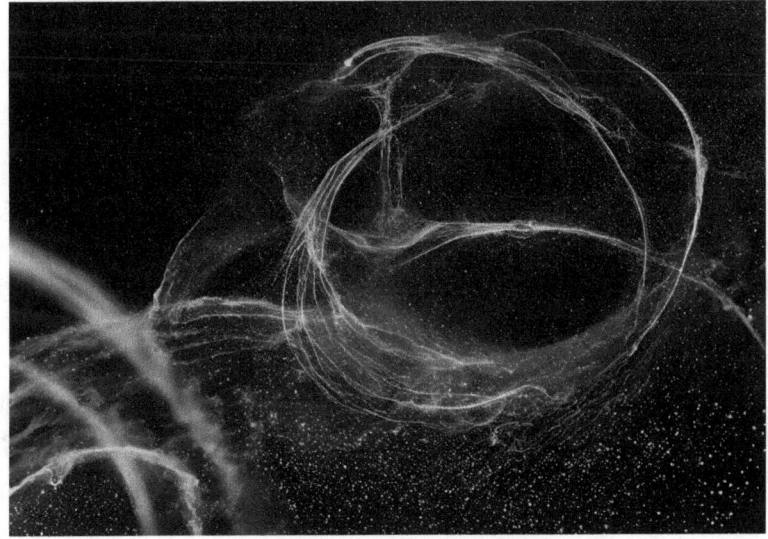

The unified field is the source of all things.[38]

The unified field is the source of all things. It is where all of life and its phenomena come from and to where it all returns. This field is pure potential, with nothing fixed unless and until you fix your attention on one probability, disregarding the others. The unified field theory suggests that all forces and particles are really the creation of the same energy, something that spiritualists have always known long before quantum physics was a thing.

Another fascinating thing about the unified field theory is the fact that it goes beyond the limitations of duality. It's no longer this or that, but this *and* that, as Bashar, channeled by Darryl Anka, is known to say often during his sessions. All things are one and the same, varying only in frequency or degree of expression. It's like how heat and cold are really expressions of one thing: temperature. This non-duality is reflected in spiritual teachings such as Hinduism's Advaita Vedanta, or Tibetan Buddhism's Dzogchen.

Spiritual teachers such as Deepak Chopra and "the sleeping prophet," Eckhart Tolle, have shed light on the similarities between experiencing the quantum field and enlightenment. If you understand your true nature isn't your name, age, job, looks, or any other ego attachment but is actually the field itself, you'll become aware of who you really are.

You will no longer be swayed by physical reality. You'll know just how plasticky it is and never settle for anything less than you desire. Knowing yourself as and in the quantum field means discovering the true meaning of enlightenment, which is ultimately how to break free from the bonds of suffering, lack, and limitation.

## Jung's Synchronicity

If you think coincidences are a thing, think again. There are no accidents in this universe. Still not convinced? That's fine, but can you think of a time when a series of events so implausible occurred, forcing you to pause and wonder if there's not a divine, supernatural force winking at you or having fun at your expense?

Carl Jung was a brilliant mind who came up with the term synchronicity, which demonstrates there's a powerful connection between your mind and the universe. Synchronicity is about "coincidences" pregnant with meaning, at least as far as the observer is concerned.

Carl Jung stated that there is a deep connection between the physical world and your mental world.[34]

These events are a-causal, which is a fancy way of saying when it plays out, you can't point out which event was the cause and which was the effect. It would be like throwing double sixes six times in a row as soon as the clock strikes six while you're wearing a football jersey with the number six emblazoned on it. How many sixes would it take for you to realize there's nothing random about that occurrence in that example?

According to Jung, there's a deep connection between your mental world and the physical one around you. You draw information from the collective unconscious, a cloud or field from which everyone else receives insights, inspiration, vision, revelation, and more.

This collective unconscious is full of archetypes and experiences that are relatable to one and all rather than relegated to an individual's experience. These Jungiang archetypes show up in everyday life in the form of synchronistic events. What's the purpose of these events, you may wonder? Well, they're either delivering you messages or showing you what's going on in your inner, mental world.

Carl Jung didn't have much to do with quantum physics, but his work on synchronicity, upon closer inspection, shares a philosophical connection with quantum phenomena. Think about non-locality, for a moment, as particles that are linked with each other mirror each other, and you'll find how that concept parallels Jungian ideas of the connection between the world and your psyche through entanglement and the observer effect.

Did Jung specifically talk about a connection between synchronicity and the idea that all things are preordained? Not really. It was something he preferred to view with an open mind. At the most, he saw synchronicity as something of a psychic experience that deserves your rapt attention and keen study.

Still, some view synchronicity as more than meaningful coincidences, choosing to see them as messages from a higher power, the universe, or Source Energy, if you prefer. This worldview holds that synchronicity is a sign that the universe isn't the chaotic result of some random big bang but that there must be an intelligence running things, ensuring all of creation remains on a divinely ordered path.

## The Non-local Nature of Quantum Phenomena

It's not hard to find the connection between the quantum phenomena of non-locality and spiritual experiences that defy logic and aren't bound by spacetime limitations. You already understand entanglement, but what about Bell's theorem? Here's how that works.

You have a pair of dice. These are no ordinary dice, either. They're magical. Throw them, and they'll always give you the same value, regardless of how apart they are from each other in space or time. Plop one in Timbuktu and the other in Pluto, and they'd still have the same value. Transport one die to the caveman or Anunnaki era and another to the year 5078, and they'd still have the same value. *How is this any different from entanglement?*

Enter Bell's Theorem. Classical physics suggests that at some point when you throw both dice, they should have different values because non-locality isn't a logical expectation or phenomenon in macroscopic physics. Yet, when it comes to entangled particles (or, in this case, entangled dice), they'll always match each other – with no regard for the limits of classical physics.

Therefore, Bell's Theorem declares that there's no compatibility between quantum mechanics and a theory involving local hidden variables. Put simply, if the universe only functions the way classical physics dictates, then that means spooky action at a distance is impossible; but as you already know, it's not only possible but proven.

This chapter is about quantum mysticism, so it's best to circle back to the topic. Bell's Theorem and quantum entanglement have parallels with transcendent spiritual experiences. Have you ever had a moment when you felt connected to the world around you to a profound, inexplicable degree? What about a moment when it felt like time no longer existed?

During special occurrences such as these, you lose your ego. You lose awareness of everything in your mind that has you thinking you're separate from the world outside yourself. You merge with the cosmic soup of energy, becoming one with all. Moments like these show you there's a dimension of life beyond linear time. Your soul understands the first few lines of William Blake's poem, Auguries of Innocence:

*To See a World in a Grain of Sand*
*And a Heaven in a Wild Flower*
*Hold Infinity in the palm of your hand*
*And Eternity in an hour*

Not only do you lose your ego and all sense of time, but you also develop truly unconditional love and acceptance for one and all, even those you never thought you could feel compassion for. So, what do these spiritual experiences have in common with non-locality in quantum physics? They're both phenomena that take place in a realm where clocks and maps are irrelevant.

Both also reflect the interconnectedness of all life. They also demonstrate that there's something even more real than what your five senses pick up on in this physical world, which you cannot grasp, at least not with your present understanding of the universe.

## Exercises to Tap into the Unified Field

The takeaway from this chapter is there's value in maintaining your sense of unified awareness. The question is, how can you pull this off? Using the following exercise, you'll transform your life for the better through the fastest and most efficient means by shifting your experiences from the quantum level rather than through effort and fruitless action.

That's not to say action has no place in changing your life, but once you attain that unified awareness, you'll find the actions you take are less like an uphill battle and more like rowing your boat merrily downstream like life is just a dream - a lucid one that's very responsive to your thoughts, feelings, and intentions.

**Being here, now:** Find a comfy position to sit or lie in, and then close your eyes. Direct your attention to your breath. Part your lips slightly. Take a deep inhale through your nostrils, hold the breath in for a few seconds, and then exhale through your mouth. It's natural for your exhale to be longer than your inhale, so don't overthink it. Simply notice your breath. Give it a second or two before you repeat the process once more.

You could pay attention to the sound of your breathing, the feeling of the air as it goes in through your nostrils and out through your lips, the gentle rise and fall of your chest and belly, or the counts for each portion of this awareness exercise.

Do this for ten to fifteen minutes each day. You'll find it useful to have a timer set before you begin so you don't keep distracting yourself by checking to see how many minutes go by. *Let the timer do the worrying on your behalf!*

Be warned: Your mind will wander away from your breath. It could do this as many as three times every 45 seconds or a hundred times in a minute. When you notice this, it's imperative that you don't beat yourself up for losing focus. If anything, that's worth celebrating; you're learning to notice when your mind wanders!

So, gently and lovingly release the distracting thought or feeling, and return to your breathing as many times as you notice you've been distracted. With time, you'll notice you're less and less distracted.

The benefit of being mindful of the here and now through this deliberate meditation will reveal itself to you in the coming days and weeks as long as you're consistent. You'll discover the power you have within to change your world, and not only that, you'll be less reactive to the things that triggered you into undesirable states of fear, anger, and anxiety.

From this more empowered state, you can envision the life you want, hold your goal steady in your mind, and breeze through the process of transformation as life shifts from what you don't want to what you prefer.

# Chapter 7: Entanglement – Everything Is Connected

In this chapter, you'll explore the spiritual dimensions of life. Not only that, you'll learn more about the interconnectedness of all things, as demonstrated by quantum entanglement through the lens of spirit. So, are you ready to go even deeper into the rabbit hole? Good. You're going to love it!

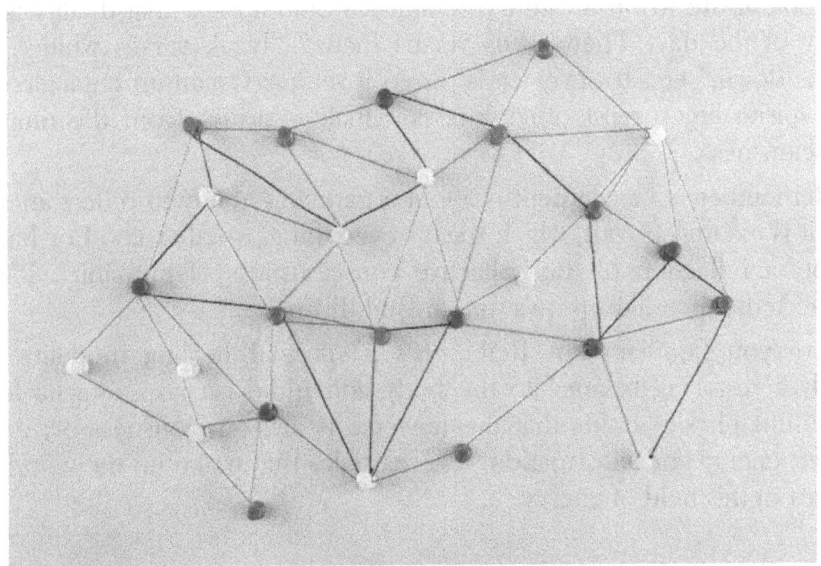

Everything is connected.[26]

# Entanglement: A Metaphor for Spiritual Interconnectedness

There are other implications of quantum entanglement outside of science. Where else can you apply the idea of two particles, separated by space, still sharing a connection so strong as to mirror each other? You'll find the theme of interconnectedness across religions - echoed in spiritual beliefs and practices. It's not simply about being at one with others and your world but being at one with the very source of all creation.

All of life is a cocreation if you really think about it. Everyone and everything has a part to play to keep life going. When you think about the observer effect and the fact that at every point in time, there are billions of points in space observing everything else, you'll realize how truly interconnected everything is.

Suddenly, the butterfly effect doesn't appear so outrageous. Every observer is doing their part to shape reality as it is, thanks to consciousness. Your intention and attention matter as much as the next person's, dovetailing perfectly together to create outcomes that match expectations, regardless of what spiritual path or practice you use to create your desired reality.

Look at the world around you, and it would appear that duality is the order of the day. There's "us versus them," "black versus white," "up versus down," etc. It never ends, or so it seems. Quantum entanglement and spirituality suggest otherwise. All duality springs from the unity of consciousness.

Remember, entanglement is about a particle's ability to reflect another one it is entangled with, which means everything, whether good or bad, is simply a reflection of the collective consciousness of humanity. It's all connected, much like Indra's web in Buddhism.

Are you familiar with Reiki? It's a spiritual healing modality that involves restoring balance to the body and mind on an energetic level. Quantum physics holds that the universe is all consciousness or, if you prefer, energy and information. The particles that make up the world are all part of this field of energy.

Practices like Reiki tap into specific healing energies from the body's bioenergetic field.[36]

In spiritual traditions and practices like Reiki, the point is to work with this field to achieve your goals since everything in the field is connected to everything else. It's all fields within fields. Your body has its bioenergetic field, and since it's connected to the unified field, it makes sense for Reiki practitioners to draw specific healing energies from that field into yours to help you heal.

## Unity in Diversity

Quantum entanglement is proof of unity in diversity. On the surface, this sentence may seem paradoxical. After all, the very essence of diversity suggests that the parts are distinct and separate from each other. Otherwise, how could you tell them apart from one another?

However, when you view life through the lens of quantum entanglement or with spiritual eyes, it becomes blatantly obvious that everything is really one and the same, regardless of how separate they may appear to be to the ordinary senses. This is not a call for you to lose your sense of self or to assume that no one or nothing is special. Your uniqueness is as valid as the fact that you are united with the world around you in energy and spirit.

Hinduism is one of those spiritual paths that emphasizes the idea of unity in diversity. If you follow this path, then you believe that Brahman is the ultimate reality that does not have any specific form. The Brahman is also infinite and beyond time, for it is both primordial and eternal. While it is the very essence from which all of life is crafted, it is also represented by the Hindu pantheon of deities, which represent its different divine aspects.

For instance, there is Shiva, who is the God of destruction and regeneration. Saraswati is the embodiment of knowledge. Lakshmi is the

Goddess who is the essence of wealth and prosperity. These are just a few of the Hindu pantheon of gods and goddesses. While Hindus respect and revere each one of these divine beings because of their unique qualities, they are seen as being part of the Brahman. In this way, Hinduism reflects the truth of quantum entanglement, which is unity in diversity.

What about the Sufis? What do they believe? Sufism is a mystical aspect of Islam. One of the tenets this philosophy espouses is the idea that all creation springs forth from the divine and contains an element of divinity within it. This is known as the unity of being or Wahdat al-Wujud.

A true Sufi will tell you that there is nothing and no one in existence that does not contain the divine creator's essence within them. All of creation is a manifestation of Allah's divinity. It is impossible for anything or anyone to exist without the will of Allah keeping them in existence.

Sufis believe in a higher order for everything to connect for existence.[27]

Have you ever heard of Indra's net? Indra is a Vedic Deva. Hanging over his palace on Mount Meru, the net has a jewel in each node. An interesting truth about these jewels is that they reflect one another. If you think about it, this is a perfect representation of the interconnectedness of everything in the world. It is a beautiful way to visualize unity in diversity.

Buddhism also has the concept of *Pratitya Samutpada*, also known as dependent origination, which emphasizes that each phenomenon, known and unknown, is not only connected to the others but also exists because of said others.

Have you ever heard of Yin and Yang? No, not the rapping twins. Yin and Yang is the Taoist concept of opposites harmonizing with each other.

While these forces are clearly distinct from each other, they depend on each other to keep the world performing in balance as it should.

Imagine a world where there's only up and no down or left and no right. That would be a rather strange world to live in, wouldn't it? Yin and Yang express the idea of unity and diversity wonderfully well by taking polar opposites that make up duality and blending them together to create a harmonious existence.

Society has brainwashed people into demonizing one end of the spectrum over the other. Extreme conservatives don't want to hear out extreme liberals because the other side is full of demons or deluded people. This is a sad way to live life because even a broken clock gets it right at some point during the day.

Then there's the argument over what's more superior, the masculine or the feminine. In a world that does not recognize or respect unity in diversity, you get Andrew Tate at one extreme and Shera Seven at the other. Being unable to find the balance between light and dark is a recipe for disaster, and in case you wondered, "dark" in this context is not a bad thing. That thought process would be akin to saying the night and moon are evil and the day and sun are good.

There will always be those who argue that everything is one, and that's all there is to it. Then you have those who argue the opposite, claiming that it's ridiculous at best to suggest everyone's one and the same and invalidating at worst. This is the lovely thing about quantum entanglement, as it acts as a bridge between both philosophies. It demonstrates that the universe, while fundamentally united, is a space that allows diversity and uniqueness to thrive. The whole is not greater than the sum of its parts, and vice versa, as one can't exist without the other.

# Meditation and Contemplation: Bridges to Quantum Power

How do you take advantage of quantum entanglement? If two particles are interconnected on a quantum level, affecting each other instantaneously, it stands to reason that you could achieve the same thing with your life. Think of yourself as a particle and your experience of life as another particle with which you are intricately connected.

Up until this point, you may have allowed the external reflection of your life experience to dictate your state of being. However, since you are entangled with your life experience, what if you simply switch your state of being without waiting for the world outside of you to do so first?

For instance, if you want more happiness and rewarding relationships in your life, what if rather than waiting for people to show up who are a perfect fit for your desires, you embody the state of being a person who already has these fulfilling connections?

According to the principle of quantum entanglement, your life will have to reflect this brand-new state of being that you have adopted. The most effective way to take advantage of this power is to become deeply aware of your connection with the world around you. It must sink from basic head knowledge into your heart or feeling center and head down into your belly: *you are not separate from everyone else.*

When it's "in your belly," you live your life consciously aware of the other parts of yourself. It's easy to assume that simply accepting this truth in your mind is enough, but that's not the case. You need to really get this down in your gut. How do you accomplish this? Through the mechanisms of meditation and contemplation.

Meditation makes your experience of oneness and unity very real and palpable. You can't meditate for three hours straight once every four business months and assume that should get the job done. It's much better to be consistent with your practice. Even just five minutes a day will help you become more aware of your connection to all things, and with time, you'll carry that awareness even after you've finished sitting in silence.

Many practitioners of meditation report experiencing a point when it feels like they expand beyond or collapse into their bodies, becoming everything or nothing. You get the sense that there's no way to tell where you end and the world begins. Words can only do so much to capture the profound experience of unity that comes through meditation. You have to put in the work and see for yourself.

Contemplation is another powerful tool similar to meditation. When you meditate, you deliberately release your thoughts and feelings, observing them with no attachment. However, when you contemplate, you take time to ponder specific topics. The goal of contemplation is to receive deep, profound insight and understanding regarding your spiritual walk.

By giving your mind the task of unpacking the idea of quantum entanglement, you reveal your manifestation power to yourself. Quantum entanglement suggests that all things are interconnected, which would imply that if you want something, you already have it since you are that which you desire.

Remember: *Tat tvam asi.* "You are that." The seeker is the sought. Awaken to the truth that you contain all you want and need, and you no longer have to seek these things out. Your desires will find you. This is just one of many realizations you arrive at when you practice contemplation.

## Quantum Meditation

Quantum meditation is no ordinary form of meditation because it involves working with quantum physics principles. The way to work with this meditation modality is to accept that your thoughts, feelings, and intentions have real effects on your experience of life. The process of thinking and feeling interacts with the quantum field.

Remember, this field is full of potential, which means that your thoughts and feelings are your observations of the field. Your observations, in turn, crystallize a specific, matching outcome out of the many probabilities the field offers you. So meditation not only helps you with manifestation but also reminds you that you are eternally connected to the quantum field, making it easier for you to manifest your heart's desires.

How do you incorporate the principles of quantum physics in a practical way as you meditate? Consider the observer effect and you'll understand the importance of using your imagination to visualize the preferred version of yourself you prefer. You will also be working with the power of intention to supercharge your visualization.

*Intention* is your will. It is knowing that not only is your preferred reality possible but also a done deal. With this attitude, you will influence your physical reality so it mirrors the visions that you have in your mind of how it should be.

A powerful goal of quantum meditation is to enable you to feel oneness with the universe. More often than not, when people meditate, it's because they're looking for ways to alleviate feelings of anxiety, depression, worry, etc. People meditate to find inner peace.

However, quantum meditators seek much more than stillness. They want to experience the life that they know they deserve to live.

Even when they don't have a specific desire they'd like to bring into this 3D reality, quantum meditators continue their practice to remind themselves of the interconnectedness of all things and remain in the awareness of their unity with "the all," or the unified field, if you prefer.

Quantum meditation is a combination of mindfulness and quantum physics principles that lead you to a state of superconsciousness. Here's how to use quantum meditation to accomplish whatever your heart desires.

**Make a decision.** You must know exactly what you want from life. Far too many people are well-versed in what they don't want. In fact, you may have answered the question, "What do you want?" by rapidly reeling off everything you can think of that you'd like to stop or end or wish wasn't a problem for you. If this is the case, you're focused on the wrong end of the stick.

To make this more practical, you shouldn't be saying you want a better-paying job than the one you have when what you really want is more money for less work. If you're not clear about what you want yet, you can use the things you don't want to give you clues about what you *do* want. Then, go a step further by asking yourself why you want those things, and you'll discover your true desires.

For instance, you think you want a lot of money, but when you drill further, you realize what you really want is to travel the world. You assumed you'd need a lot of money to pull off exploring the world's beautiful treasures when that isn't true. What if all your flights, accommodations, meals, and miscellaneous needs were sorted out by someone else? So, get specific about what you want, and you'll get out of your own way.

**Get comfortable.** Find somewhere quiet, free from distractions and disturbances, where you can focus for the next 10 to 15 minutes. Make sure you're dressed comfortably so your clothes don't feel like they're itchy, too tight, too warm, etc.

Sit comfortably. Do you have a recliner? That's perfect. Set it to a semi-upright position. If you don't have one, it's fine. Sit on a chair or *on* the floor on a mat in a lotus or half-lotus position.

Close your eyes and bring your attention to your breath. Take a few deep inhales and exhales, focusing on releasing all tension and worry as you exhale. Keep breathing like this until you notice you're feeling calm and still, fully present in the here and now.

**Imagine.** This is the same thing as visualization. Picture yourself in a quantum zone. You can make it look like whatever you want it to. It could be a white or black void or the beach. It could even be a hallway full of doors that branch off to different versions of your life.

Whatever you visualize, know that this zone is where everything and anything is possible. This is the zone where every possible version of you exists. There are no limits here to the choices you could make. You can select various timelines and parallel realities. Ensure you are imagining from a first-person perspective rather than third-person. In other words, you shouldn't be seeing your body as separate from you. You should be within your body.

Imagine that multiple versions of reality branch out from your present one. Whatever you do, don't be in a hurry to choose the closest or quickest. Instead, select the path that you desire the most. This means you'll have to check logic at the door. The quantum zone is beyond logic and rationality. You'd be doing yourself a great disservice by binding yourself to these things.

**Choose.** Pick the version of your life that calls to you the loudest, the one that feels right in your soul. The process of choosing could look however you want it to. It could be you walking through a door, portal, or liminal space of some sort. It could look like flicking through channels on a television to find the version of reality you prefer and then stepping through the screen to embody that life. The choice is yours.

**Use your imaginal senses.** Once you step into the version of life that you prefer, use your 5 senses in your imagination to make everything feel real to you. What can you see in this scene? What do you hear? What can you smell, taste, and touch? How do you feel emotionally? The deeper you immerse yourself in your imaginal senses, the more real it will feel to you and the more you charge this new version of your life, forcing it to become your new normal.

**Accept it is done.** Resist the temptation to dismiss this exercise as "nothing more than imagination" when you've finished. Imagination is a tool that allows you to interact with the quantum field and pull from it whatever you desire. Those teachers and other adults who reprimanded you for daydreaming as a child owe you a million apologies.

There is an important point to remember if you decide to practice quantum meditation to manifest your dreams. Whatever you do, you should imagine the different options available to you *long after* you have received your desire.

If you want to get a car, you don't imagine yourself at the dealership trying different vehicles on for size. Instead, you imagine yourself, say, six days, weeks, months, or a year after you've got the vehicle. This way, you fix it firmly in your mind that your desire is no longer a desire – but is the reality of your situation right now. As the great mystic Neville Goddard put it, you're making "there" here and "then" now.

You can use this quantum meditation technique for whatever you want. You could use it for relationships, friendships, promotions, and healing. Did you have a terrible night? Were you unable to sleep long enough? You can use this meditation to place yourself in a version of reality where you got the best night's sleep and you'll be amazed at how effectively this works.

Working with the quantum field through this form of meditation changes the neurochemical workings of your brain, putting you in touch with the power to choose rather than roll over and accept the hand fate has dealt you. Through quantum meditation, you'll come to recognize your interconnectedness to the world and become more aware of your consciousness. This is how you heal your life. This is how you manifest your dreams.

# Chapter 8: Superposition: Anything Is Possible

Superposition is quite a paradox, isn't it? Imagine particles are like ice cream flavors. How interesting would it be to have the same scoop be every flavor imaginable at the same time? In this chapter, you'll dive deeper into the idea of superposition to understand how it works even better and find the connection between this quantum physics phenomenon and spiritual concepts like the power of focused attention and intention.

## Superposition: Unlimited Potential

Schrödinger's cat thought experiment is the epitome of superposition. Remember, it's about a quantum system being able to exist in more states than one until the observer effect kicks in. This is still a bit difficult to accept because it would imply that the red car in your driveway is also orange, yellow, blue, green, purple, upside down, broken down, brand new, and also *not* in your driveway unless you're looking at it. So, what does superposition have to do with spirituality?

Regardless of the spiritual path you consider, which culture it's from, or from which period of humanity's history it originated, you'll find there's a belief that every person carries a spark of divinity within, which gives them value. Spirituality suggests everyone has inherent worth, thanks to this *divine spark*, as the Christians call it.

In Buddhism, this spark is *Buddha nature*. In Hinduism, it's the *Atman*, a word to describe the true self. In Islam, it's the *fitra*, the part of human nature that honors the *tawhid* or oneness of God. This part of you is primordial purity. By embracing these spiritual tenets, you learn that it makes no sense to pigeonhole yourself with labels. These are concepts that show you that you're far more than your physical self.

You have the potential to be, do, or have all that you can imagine and then some, but it's all going to remain dormant until you choose to express that potential within you, whether spiritually, emotionally, intellectually, or in any other way.

Superposition in quantum mysticism invites you to move from black-and-white thinking to play more in the gray. Ditch the limitations of "either/or" and embrace "this *and* that." This way, you'll become aware of the various abilities, skills, talents, and experiences available to you and choose what you want from that smorgasbord for a fuller, richer life.

If you've lived long enough, you've probably come to accept that life will always have ups and downs, good and bad, highs and lows. All of these things are ultimately good because you evolve and grow by experiencing both sides of the spectrum. In the darkness, you discover new aspects of yourself, just as you do when it's light.

As a result, you become aware of what's possible for you. When this happens, you can't go back to being who you used to be without feeling miserable and unfulfilled. It's best to stretch and grow beyond that. As the process of observing a super-positioned particle forces a collapse in its wave function, it assumes a specific state, and so do the experiences in your life compel you to embody and express the part of you that was once no more than a dream.

Many people find themselves up in arms about what they're supposed to do with themselves. What's the point of life? Why go on? These, and many more, are some of the existential questions that humanity's forced to ask of itself. How do you know you're supposed to be a pilot instead of a pirate? How do you know you're meant to be a matchmaker rather than a manager? Well, you don't. You're not "supposed" to do anything other than explore yourself for the rest of your life. That's it.

Self-exploration and self-expression are the ultimate reasons for living. You can't fight the thing within you asking you to grow in one direction or the other. Try as you might, change is inevitable. When you make peace with exploring beyond your comfort zone, you'll learn more about who you are. Your true self is full of wonderful, sometimes mind-bending surprises if only you keep an open mind and maintain your affinity for falling down rabbit holes. Your inspired thoughts and ideas are in a superposition state and will remain there until you act on them. Only then can you bring them into reality and see how you like it.

The concept of manifestation is a popular one in spirituality. You could think of manifestation as the process of bringing forth your quantum desires into the physical world to experience them. Until your desire becomes a reality, it remains in a state of superposition.

So, you can look at the quantum phenomenon of superposition as a metaphor for the potential that you carry within you, which is yet untapped and unlimited. Your desires remain in the quantum realm unless you choose to manifest them and make them real in the physical plane. Manifestation is the ultimate form of creativity.

You now understand what superposition is about. How do you take advantage of it? How do you put it to work? To create the life of your dreams, the first thing you must do is accept that everything is possible. Just because you do not see a path to the preferred outcome you desire right now does not mean there isn't one or that you can't have what you want.

In the same way that the quantum particle exists in a myriad of states simultaneously, you also have a myriad of ideas that exist within you.

There is a version of you with that car, house, significant other, or whatever else you seek. There is a version of you that is healthier than the current version you're embodying. There is a version of you that lives a fulfilled life and has finally found true love. Whoever you wish you were, you are that person, but you are being that person *potentially,* in a state of superposition.

The way to force a wave function collapse and become this potential person you'd like to actualize is by first accepting that everything is possible so you don't limit yourself to the things you are already familiar with. Don't let logic act like a ball and chain, keeping you from spreading your wings and flying.

The next thing you must do is visualize the outcome you prefer. By developing a mental picture of how you'd feel, think, and go about your day as this person that you want to become, you force the wave function collapse to occur. You force the superposition state of your potential into becoming crystal and firm in one state only. Once you have this clear mental snapshot of yourself, you should take action. Action is another important part of the process of collapsing your super-positioned ideas and preferences into reality.

## Intention and the Potential for Personal Transformation

When you contemplate the idea of superposition, you realize there's no such thing as a fixed reality. The truth about reality is it's dynamic. There are countless possibilities that play with one another to create even more interesting possibilities. If you would like to transform your life completely, then you need to give some thought to what your conscious intentions are because they are the propellants of the change you seek.

Due to the limitless nature of the quantum realm, the change you could experience could absolutely rock your world. Limitations are only as real as you think they are. For far too long, humanity has gone about assuming that it is impossible to change reality. This assumption is further entrenched in the human psyche thanks to organizations and systems with rules and processes that must be followed to the letter.

The seeming rigidity of the nature of reality has gone unquestioned for long enough. You could think of it as a blessing that quantum physicists have discovered and continued to research the idea of superposition, which suggests that reality is as fluid as can be. It is full of infinite possibilities that continue to flow and evolve as they interact with each other in an ebb and flow.

Looking at this idea through a spiritual lens, you'll find that reality is a matter of creation, of interconnected threads that are ever in a state of flux, responding to whatever you're thinking or feeling in the moment or whatever intention you fixed in your mind.

If you desire transformation like nothing you've experienced in your life, you need to use the power of intention. At this point, the logical question to ask is, *what exactly is intention?* What does it mean? Some people think of intention as nothing more than goal setting. They think it's only about making plans and attempting to follow those plans.

An intention is much more than that. It is what gives life to transformation. It is a prayer, silent and sacred, that you whisper with sincerity to the universe or your Creator, trusting that it will be expressed as your reality.

When you express your intention, you aren't simply uttering words for the sake of them. You're bringing every part of you into play. You're infusing these words with energy or feeling.

Your intention is the one thing that you live for. It's what you wish to experience above every other thing in life. More often than not, intentions are tied to those things that you don't consider possibilities, in the sense that you may not think of the concept of intention unless and until you notice you've been struggling with a particular goal for a while. But why is that the case? To understand the answer to that question, you must think about the nature of an intention.

## Conscious Intention

For one thing, intentions are clear. Are you one of those people who consistently makes plans only to have them fall through, and you've decided that planning is an exercise in futility? It could be because you did not bring clarity into the mix from the get-go. You must be clear about what you intend to experience or accomplish first. This means tuning into what your deepest desires are.

Once you become clear, you must feed your intention with faith, which is an inherent trust that this thing you desire not only can manifest but is as good as done. To have faith is to go beyond believing to knowing that it is done. From this state of knowing you have your desire, you can then take action.

When you combine clarity, faith, and action together, you have a powerful intention that must grow and become *that which you seek in reality*. This is the secret, not-so-secret formula to creating your reality with the power of intention and transforming your life in ways beyond imagination. Your intention acts as the observer collapsing the wave function into your desired outcome.

Whether your intention is big or small is insignificant. In fact, the ideas of big and small are nothing more than logical in positions that you place upon yourself. As Abraham, a collection of entities channeled by Esther Hicks, often says, "It is as easy to create a castle as it is a button."

You would be doing yourself a huge favor by doing away with those assumptions that some things are more difficult or will take longer time than others to manifest. All you need to do is remain consistent with your intention by keeping your attention focused on what you desire and acting in alignment with that desire, assuming that you already have what you want. By doing this, your intention will blossom into an actual manifestation.

Some people understand the idea of intention and work with it to manifest their desires, but they fail. Why does that happen? There's a key piece of the puzzle that's missing, which, once you have it, will unlock the doors to the impossible for you forever. This missing piece is repetition.

Those who attempt to manifest their desires and get no results often assume that once is enough. It's possible to get to the point where things happen that fast, but when they're just starting out with learning to manifest and don't have enough faith, it's not a good idea to only work with intention now and then. If this is you, there's no reason to beat yourself up for not knowing. Repetition is powerful.

When you repeatedly restate your intentions and focus on them, you cause all your thoughts and actions to line up with the preferred version of reality that you seek. Nature abhors a vacuum. If you are thinking, acting, feeling, and living like someone who already has what you want, you are causing a vacuum, and therefore, nature must swoop in to correct that vacuum by giving you the life you're acting as if you already have.

This is quantum entanglement in action, where whatever's happening to one particle must happen to the other particle it's entangled with. Repetition is how you learn everything, isn't it? It's how you became so proficient at reading and writing. Well, the same process is how you become proficient at living your life as this new version of yourself that you are as yet unaccustomed to being. Think of it like watering a plant and applying fertilizer so that when it blooms, it blooms beautifully.

## Visualization

When you visualize, you create a powerful, clear picture in your mind of what you prefer to experience in your life. Visualization is an excellent tool to catalyze your personal growth and encourage the manifestation of your dreams. There appears to be a vast chasm between your desires, which are in a state of superposition, and the manifestation of said desires. Visualization is the bridge that connects these two together. As you picture yourself, your world, and your life being the way you'd prefer, you cause a wave function collapse.

Visualization is like selecting a specific channel on which to watch a specific show. For instance, say you'd like to watch something by the actor Ryan Reynolds. You've seen him in a plethora of comedic shows and movies, but you'd like to see a more serious side of him. So you scroll through all the options of everything he's ever been in, and you finally choose the one thing where he plays a serious character.

You know this is different because you can see a visual representation of Ryan Reynolds being serious versus being goofy. When it comes to manifesting your desires, you are Ryan Reynolds in this context. You are also the person with the remote control who gets to choose which show you'd like to see. You accomplish this using visualization. Visualization is powerful when it is repeated. Each time, you keep your focus on the version of yourself you would prefer to be.

As you visualize, you should never imagine yourself being projected on a screen; instead, embody yourself by seeing through your own eyes. Some people have used visualization and found it doesn't work for them, but for others because whenever they practice visualization, someone else winds up with their manifestation.

If you practice visualization by looking at yourself as if you're on a screen, you are projecting your desires onto someone else. But by embodying yourself, looking through your eyes, and being inside your body as you visualize your preferred outcome, you ensure that your manifestation is yours and yours alone.

## Affirmations

Affirmations are statements made in the present sense to attest to the fact that you already have whatever it is you want. Superposition offers the perfect metaphor to understand how affirmations can crystallize into actual manifestations in your life. Every word that you speak is a seed that must bear fruit sooner or later.

The Bible says life and death are in the power of the tongue. While that may sound like an utterly dramatic statement, it is not far from the truth because often, as the Bible also says, out of the abundance of the heart, the mouth speaks. Whatever you truly believe about yourself, your life, and others is exactly what you'll say unless you're deliberately trying to deceive someone or actively changing your life through the power of your words.

A key part of affirmations is repetition. As you repeat these affirmations, you cause your subconscious mind to buy into them more and more each day. You are causing the wave function collapse that will convert your present reality into the desired one. As you repeatedly affirm your preferred truths, you'll discover that your actions and thoughts are in alignment with these new statements.

You're missing out if you don't take advantage of the power of affirmations because there's no better way to change your belief systems. Now the question is, why would you want to change what you believe? The answer is simple. You can't manifest what you don't believe. An excellent definition of a belief, according to Abraham Hicks, is it's a thought that you've been thinking over and over long enough that you now think it's the truth.

A key part of that definition is the idea of repetition. If you have installed beliefs in your mind that do not serve you and will not help you accomplish the dreams that you want to see become real, you would be doing yourself a favor by working with affirmations that support your new preferred life. If you'd like a different experience, then you have to install a new belief system, and there's no better way to accomplish that than by using repeated affirmations consistently.

The moment you adopt new beliefs is when life will shift for you. This is because your beliefs act as a filter. So if you believe that life is full of hostile and terrible people, the kindest person in the world could pass by you on the street, smile at you, and say hello, and you would somehow find a way to misinterpret that greeting as being malicious. Once you believe differently that life is full of wonderful, genuine, kind people, you'll begin noticing more of that in your life because you have a new filter that supports a life full of pleasant people around you.

Now that you understand the power of conscious intention, visualization, and affirmation, here is an entry-level process that incorporates these tools to manifest your reality:

- **Set clear** and precise descriptions of what you desire.
- **Set an intention** framed in the present tense based on your desire. Keep it short and simple.
- **Relax.** Close your eyes, and get comfortable. Breathe deeply until you are aware of only the present moment, and then imagine yourself doing, being, or having whatever you desire.
- **Repeat positive affirmations** that speak to the truth of what you desire as being real. Do this at least once a day for five to ten minutes at a time, either at the start or at the end of your day.

Your affirmation is your intention in words. Keep each one short and simple, and always start with the words "I am." If your conscious mind keeps butting in with logic, telling you that you aren't who you say you are, you can use "ask affirmations" instead. How?

Ask yourself questions like, "How did I become so wealthy?" "How did I become so healthy?" You're not asking these questions to get actual answers. You're only asking them the same way you'd ask your significant other, "How did I get so lucky to be with you?" Whether you're using *ask*firmations or *aff*irmations, repeat them over and over with feeling and gratitude.

- **Act in alignment with your intention to the best of your abilities.** Eventually, ideas will spring up within you about which course of action to take next. Follow every hunch you receive. Act with the awareness that it's already done, and even if your action does not prove fruitful, assume that it's already done.

Just because you walk into a movie theater while the protagonist is down and out doesn't necessarily mean that's how the movie ends. If you've already seen the movie before, you're not bothered by that one sad frame. You know the good guys come out on top in the end. This is the same attitude you should approach your experiences as you set about the business of manifesting your dreams.

It should offer you some comfort to know that there is a version of yourself who already has everything you could ever dream of and has an entirely different set of desires and goals that they'd like to accomplish. This version exists not only because of the quantum phenomenon of superposition but also the fact that the multiverse is a sound theory. Not even Zuckerberg's metaverse, with all his smarts and dollars poured into it, could ever hold a candle to the supernatural multiverse.

# Chapter 9: The Multiverse

According to the Many-Worlds interpretation of quantum mechanics, the multiverse is real. Every quantum event could lead to a myriad of outcomes, and each of these outcomes causes a separate branch of reality to be formed. So, in this final chapter of the book, you are going to delve deeper into the multiverse. You'll understand the ins and outs of this theory and see how it can reshape your assumptions of life for the better.

The multiverse.[38]

## The Multiverse

According to the hypothesis of the multiverse, the world is full of multiple universes besides the one in which you currently live. Some of these universes may closely mirror what you're familiar with, while others could be so far removed from anything that you've ever known or imagined.

The multiverse theory suggests there's a world in which gravity works in reverse; you breathe in carbon dioxide to breathe out oxygen, and the digestion process works from the bottom to the top. That last example is, granted, a little disgusting, but that's the multiverse for you. There are no limitations, and there's no such thing as "impossible" because this is a quantum theory with principles that suggest it's a valid one, while yet unproven.

There are four possible kinds of multiverses that you could experience.

1. The inflationary multiverse.
2. The quilted multiverse.
3. The quantum multiverse.
4. The brane multiverse.

**The Inflationary Multiverse:** Do you remember The Big Bang Theory? No, not the show, the actual theory that the birth of the universe was the result of a Big Bang. After this phenomenon, the whole universe began to inflate like a balloon or a bubble. Scientists say that ever since the Big Bang, the universe has been expanding outward.

If the inflationary multiverse is a thing, this begs the question, is every universe out there also in the process of expansion? According to the theory, the multiverse is a field of energy. This field is infinite and ever-expanding, full of universes that are also in the process of expanding. For this to be possible, the field of energy obviously must exist beyond the limitations of space and time. Scientists also suggest that each of the bubbles or universes may have their own unique laws of physics.

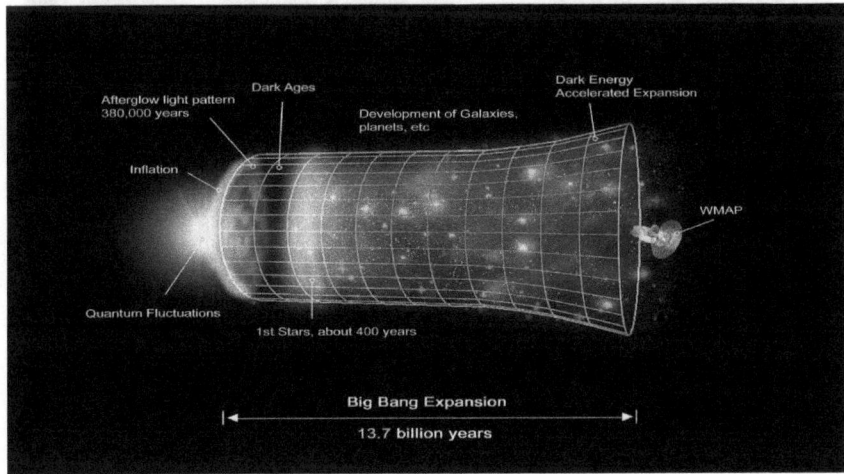

**The Multiverse.**

**The Quilted Multiverse:** This multiverse is actually one universe, but it's infinite. The question is, what is the degree of its infinity? Scientists suggest that if you were somehow to develop the means to explore the infinity of this quilted multiverse, you would find a galaxy with a planet that has someone exactly like you on it, doing exactly what you are doing right now.

The space within the quilted multiverse is so infinite that it can house all kinds of probabilities, from the ones closest to your reality to the vastly dissimilar ones. Before you ask, yes, there's definitely a "Potterverse" and a Game of Thrones universe according to this take on the multiverse.

If this is true, why is it that (for now) it seems impossible for you to make your way outside of your zone of existence? The universe is ever-expanding in every direction. Also, there's nothing that travels faster than light. Even if you had always traveled at the same speed of light since the start of your existence in your universe, you'd never be able to travel outside of your world.

**The Quantum Multiverse:** The quantum world, as you already know, is a world full of quirks and strangeness. The laws of classical physics are so skewed that quantum physics had to be developed to explain the strange phenomena observed at this level of existence.

**The Quantum Multiverse.**

You're already familiar with some of these strange happenings like quantum entanglement, superposition, the observer effect, etc. This is a multiverse that is highly influenced by your observations, choices, and intentions.

**The Brane Multiverse:** Conjure a three-dimensional book in your mind. Now, see that book as having two-dimensional pages. According to this view of the multiverse, your universe is only one of these pages in your imaginary book.

**The Brane Multiverse.**

Now imagine that same book, but make it 10-dimensional this time. What's really happening, according to this theory, is that the universe exists on something called a brane or a membrane. This universe is an intrinsic part of all 10 dimensions of your imaginary book.

What about the other pages of your book? Well, those are other universes. According to this theory, it's possible to have black holes within the pages that act as portals that can send you to another page or universe. Some say these portals can transport you to another "book" entirely, with its own infinite pages of universes and black holes.

**What about bubble universes?** This is a unique model. Your universe is really in a false vacuum, which is a state of energy that's not stable. It's possible for pockets of "true" vacuum, which have much lower energy, to form bubble universes within your regular, physical world, where the laws of physics don't line up with the classical laws. It's possible to never stumble upon these pockets of wonky reality, let alone communicate with any life within it.

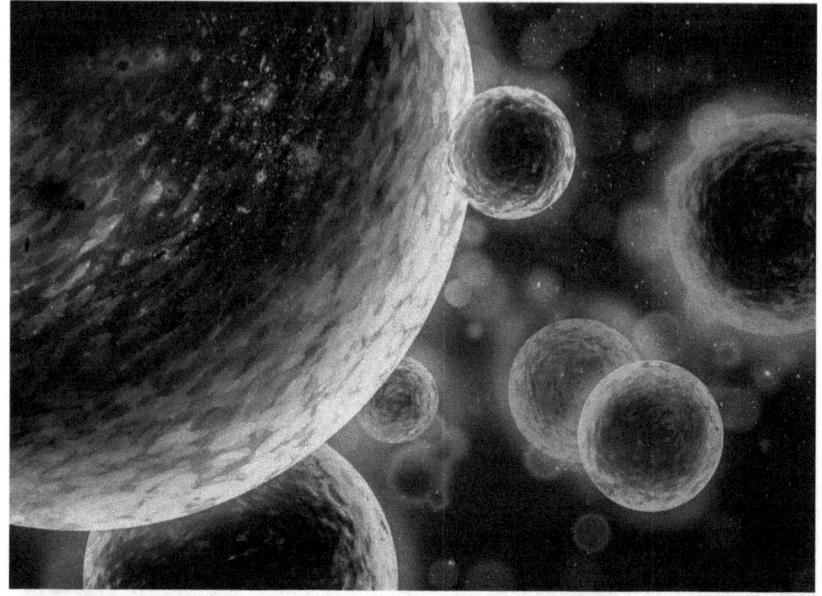

The Bubble Universe.

## String Theory: Extra Dimensions

According to string theory, it is quite possible that there are other dimensions- aside from the ones you already know – that exist in the three-dimensional world in which you live. It implies other dimensions that do not adhere to time as you know it either. String theory proposes that each of these universes has different laws of physics specifically tied to the nature of these unknown and unfamiliar dimensions. It is thanks to these extra dimensions that scientists can figure out certain inconsistencies that pop up in physics and also combine gravity with other fundamental forces in a cohesive manner.

One interesting thing about these extra dimensions, according to string theory, is that they appear to be curled up on microscopic scales infinitesimally smaller than an atom. According to scientists, it is this compact size that explains why you don't observe these extra dimensions in your daily life.

These dimensions aren't curled up randomly either but are in specific sizes and shapes. You can think of little circles or complex-looking shapes.

Sacred geometry is a part of this topic, but it is beyond the scope of this book. However, that's a subject worth diving into when you have the time.

The extra dimensions can be set up in various configurations. Each configuration is a unique one that distinctly matches a special universe with its own constants and variables. The number of potential universes you could find in the string theory landscape is astronomical and unimaginable. String theory is the womb from which the multiverse emerges.

## Implications of the Multiverse

What if the multiverse is really real? What are the implications for humanity? How will that affect the way people think of reality, consciousness, and the concept of free will? The process of pondering the idea of the multiverse, let alone accepting it, opens up a Pandora's box of unimaginable implications and questions.

If everyone other than quantum physicists were to pause and reflect on this for longer than 5 to 10 minutes a day, it would probably cause the economy to come to a crashing halt. At the very least, it would force many people to question the point of their existence on this planet.

One of the most challenging and immediately observable implications of the multiverse theory is that if the multiverse is a real thing, it would suggest that so many different life forms are yet to be discovered and probably never will be.

It would appear that aliens are a thing. It would also suggest that there's no such thing as a fixed history since every single quantum event leads to countless opportunities that branch off into new universes. For too long, people have viewed the universe through anthropocentric lenses. But what if there are actually alternative realities besides the one about which you are so knowledgeable?

Now, move on to the topic of consciousness. Is consciousness a truly universal phenomenon, or is that something that's localized? According to the many worlds' interpretations of the multiverse and other interpretations, there are an infinite number of copies of yourself in parallel worlds. They all have their unique struggles and traits.

This begs the question, what does it mean to be yourself versus your other selves? Also, is it possible that, as depicted in the Oversoul Trilogy books by Jane Roberts, there is a universal consciousness that underlies all these versions of yourself? What if you aren't the whole story or person?

What if you're only a part of a larger, grander version of yourself, much like one cell in your body does not make up your entire biological system? Can you see how this makes the problem of consciousness even harder?

Following from the previous paragraph, you have to wonder whether or not free will is real. Is your entire life already predetermined? In that case, what's the point in making plans and trying to see them through? Or do you actually have choices? Think about it. If it turns out that your universe is only one out of countless universes that already have outcomes that are set in stone, then does free will actually exist?

Do you truly have the power of choice? Some great minds suggest that if the multiverse is real, this could actually add to your free will rather than take away from it. They suggest if there are multiple versions of yourself and they're all selecting different paths of life, that can only give you even more choices as your potential increases, and you have a wider range of experiences that, even if you haven't actualized them yet, remain accessible to you in their super-positioned, potential form.

## Spirituality and Science: Bridging the Gap

The multiverse isn't the brainchild of quantum physics. Humanity has contemplated this idea for millennia. Science is only beginning the journey of proving the existence of this multiverse theory. For now, all you can rely on is the subjective evidence of the multiverse that is offered to you through spirituality.

There are countless tales of people who have successfully shifted from one reality to another and have subjective evidence. Unfortunately, science is a field that scoffs at anything anecdotal. Hopefully, scientists will find something objective that proves the multiverse is indeed real. For now, you will have to make peace with exploring how ancient philosophers, cultures, and traditions viewed the idea of many worlds.

Anaximander was a Greek philosopher from the 6th century BCE who considered the idea of an infinite "apeiron," from which everything in existence springs. Granted, his thought was not necessarily about the multiverse, but it did confirm that there might be some other reality that births this physical one.

There is also the idea of the One and the Many. According to Plato's Theory of Forms, there is a world of forms that remain unchanging because they are perfect. Forms serve as molds or archetypes from which the world as you know it was created – and is still being created. He referred to this perfect world of forms as "the One" and the imperfect world, where you exist and perceive the creations of the One as "the Many." This is yet another idea from ancient Greece that suggests there is more than one reality.

Make your way over to India and study Vedic cosmology. Comb through ancient Indian texts and analyze the Vedas, and you'll notice that there are descriptions of universes that are cyclical in nature. According to these texts, these universes create themselves only to dissolve and then be recreated. If you think about it, this almost mirrors the idea of there being countless universes with their unique traits. Hindus believe that there is one true reality underlying all of existence. This reality is known as unity. It is the Brahman that gives birth to the physical world as you know it. The physical world, according to the Hindus, is the world of Maya or illusions.

In the Chinese concept of Dao, there is a formless principle that encompasses all of existence. This principle is akin to the unified field theory of quantum physics, where everything exists in a state of potential, waiting for a waveform collapse to become one thing rather than remain all things. Traditional Chinese philosophy recognizes that there are multiple realms besides the physical world, spiritual and otherwise.

What about indigenous and shamanistic beliefs? Those who adhere to this way of life understand that there are other worlds besides this physical one. In fact, they journey to these other worlds using shamanistic practices. Some people have out-of-body experiences and lucid dreams where they travel to these mystical places. Others make use of psychedelics or other substances to get them there.

Still others employ different modalities, such as singing, dancing, chanting, and drumming, to get to these alternate universes, often returning with useful insight, revelations, guidance, and more for those who need such assistance.

It is important to include shamanistic and indigenous opinions and experiences in this book because, despite all the other theories postulated, shamans and similar people have actual evidence of other realms, even if their experiences are subjective. There are so many tales of people entering into different realms through dreams or the aforementioned modalities only to return with critical life-saving (or life-changing) information. These are well documented, so it boggles the mind why scientific society remains so brazenly dismissive of these accounts to date.

There truly is only one way to prove to yourself that there's more to life than meets the eye. What's that? You need to have your experience of these so-called subjective, nonexistent, yet unproven dimensions of existence. You could do this in many ways, but among the safest methods are lucid dreaming and out-of-body experiences.

If you have no idea where to start, you should definitely check out Robert Monroe's series on astral projection, where he shared his experiences in great detail, offering you some perspective on what to expect when you begin your journeys. The wonderful thing about Monroe's work is that he conducted his experiments and research in a scientific manner, so you can finally shut the inner cynic within you and take the plunge to discover what lies beyond the veil.

When you finally prove to yourself that there are worlds beyond the one you are familiar with, you'll open up your mind to the thought that there is indeed a version of you who already is exactly the person you would like to be. You'll also see how you can become what they are.

Remember, the multiple versions of yourself are not unlike quantum leap entangled particles. By focusing your attention on what you hope to accomplish in life and seeing yourself as having already done that, you will mirror the version of yourself who has already attained success. Your life will have no choice but to reflect to you the inner work or inner shift you've accomplished as a result.

# Conclusion

At the start of this book, you were promised a lot of weirdness. And you must admit, every page delivered on that promise. Quantum physics is the most counterintuitive thing you'll ever encounter – other than spirituality, of course. Every phenomenon in theory in this field of study is absolutely mind-boggling and forces you to pause and reflect on what you think you know about your life. Whatever you do, don't let your exploration of quantum physics end with this book. The deeper you dive into the topic, the more you will experience paradigm shifts that will benefit you in every way you can imagine.

Before you move on to reading something else, you should take time to reflect on what you've learned from these pages so far. Consider the fact that this whole time, you may have assumed that you are nothing more than a passive observer of your life. Perhaps, like many others, for the longest time, you thought that you had no control or say over how your days should go. You figured you had to eat whatever slop was served on your plate, not knowing that you could treat yourself to an entire buffet if you wanted it. With your newfound knowledge of the observer effect, you no longer have to stand by as a passive witness in your life.

You no longer have to settle. If you want something better for yourself, you absolutely can go for it because you now know that you are a conscious co-creator with the universe. You now understand that if the universe is indeed predetermined, it is at least predetermined by your observation, intention, and will. You now understand how constantly observing the same old thing gives you more of the same old thing. No longer will you allow life and its many vicissitudes to walk all over you. Instead, you take your place as a god of sorts and dictate how your life goes.

With your knowledge of superposition, you break free from the classic black-and-white thinking. As a result, you put yourself in a state where you can experience quantum shifts. According to classical physics, you should go from the first gear to the second, the third, and then the fourth. However, according to quantum physics, you can simply skip from the first to the umpteenth.

Too many people are held back in life by their rigid thinking, by their assumption that everything must happen in a logical sequence, and that it is impossible for a thing to play out in any other way than what is conventionally known and accepted. You are no longer among this class of people. You have now been set free. You recognize you have access to a world of infinite possibilities, and you will milk that opportunity to live a rich, fulfilled life for all its worth.

If you take the time to contemplate what you've learned from this book, you'll discover that there is power in focusing your attention on whatever you desire. You'll learn not to be swayed or dissuaded by the physical reality which appears to be in contrast with your desires.

Your confidence in your ability to get what you desire or even better will come from the fact that you now know all you have to do is keep your intention sure and strong – and continue to act in line with it. Above everything else, you'll recognize the artificial and unnecessary nature of the divisions that keep people from realizing that, at the end of the day, everyone is made of "star stuff," and everyone's one and the same, imbued with the power of the creator of all things.

# Part 2: Higher Consciousness

*Awakening the Power Within, Expanding Spiritual Awareness, and Elevating Conscious Living*

# Introduction

This book will help you to establish a connection to higher consciousness. It is a road map full of valuable information that you will constantly return to as your spiritual life evolves because you'll pick up something new each time you read it.

You may have suspected for the longest time that there is much more to life than meets the eye, and *you're right.* In these pages, you'll find evidence to support your suspicions – and then some.

With this book, you'll blast your eyes wide open (your third eye included) to discover the truth about existence. You'll also wake up the power you carry within you and transform your life into the one you've always dreamed of.

If you're a skeptic about how life works, the groundbreaking discoveries made in the field of quantum physics will be sure to convince you. All your doubts about the creation of reality will be completely cleared up, with everything put into its proper perspective. No longer will you dismiss the law of attraction and other laws of the Universe as mere "woo-woo" talk, especially as you practice what you learn and see the results for yourself.

Unlike other books, this book is written in simple English. You won't be baffled by language or terminology that is difficult to understand. It's one of the most accessible books on consciousness and awakening. Every page is full of powerful, transformational information that will change you, written in a transformational yet comprehensible way.

Loaded with a generous amount of hands-on instructions and methods to help you attain spiritual enlightenment, this is a book that you can't afford to ignore. You'd never deliberately rob yourself of the opportunity of a lifetime, and that's why you'll not only read this book but apply its principles to all you do.

Are you prepared to unlock the doors to wisdom? Do you think you can handle true power? Are you prepared to leave behind everything that has weighed you down and embrace a future full of joy and satisfaction?

All you have to do is walk through the gates to the true reality, leaving behind the world of illusions to find the power that's been waiting within you all this time. So, take a moment to say goodbye to your old self. Your journey to discovering your glorious, Divine Self begins with the first chapter.

# Chapter 1: What Is Higher Consciousness?

If you hang around people who dedicate their lives to practicing spirituality long enough, you'll hear the phrase "higher consciousness." But what is it? Is it a being? Is it something ephemeral? Is it somewhere out there over the rainbow or in the depths of your soul? Is it something you need to get or something you *already have?* Is it about being a genius and expressing unparalleled levels of creativity?

What is higher consciousness?[29]

No matter how many questions are swirling around in your mind, your thoughts will be a lot clearer by the end of this book. This first chapter will introduce you to what higher consciousness is. It will show you the different ways to attain this form of consciousness and explain how people connect with it, so the next time you hear your New Age friend or some spiritual teachers say, "higher consciousness," there'll be no doubt in your mind about what they mean.

## Consciousness and Its Connection to Quantum Physics

When you're "conscious," you're aware. If you think about it, you're always aware of something. You're aware that you're reading this book. You're aware of the room you're in. You're *conscious* of who you are.

So, a simplistic interpretation of consciousness is the awareness of being. As the late, great Neville Goddard once put it:

> *"The very center of consciousness is the feeling of I AM. I may forget who I am, where I am, what I am, but I cannot forget that I AM. The awareness of being remains, regardless of the degree of forgetfulness of who, where, and what I am."*

For centuries, scientists, psychologists, philosophers, and spiritualists have gone back and forth on what consciousness is. Neville's explanation is one of the easiest to grasp. If you hit your head and lose your memory, forgetting everything you've ever known, you'd at least know you exist.

In this make-believe situation where you've forgotten it all, you'll probably ask, "Who am I? Where am I?" Pay close attention to those questions, and you'll notice you definitely know you are. You experience "I Am" by being aware that you *are*.

Many philosophers over the years have offered their opinions on what consciousness is. The 17th-century philosopher René Descartes once came up with the following theory: Cogito, ergo sum, which means *"I think, therefore I am."* What Descartes's dictum suggests is anyone who's able to think has consciousness.

Ask a psychologist, and they'll tell you that consciousness is a state where you are aware of your surroundings, emotions, thoughts, and feelings. You are about to perceive these things and think about them, as well. This is your subjective experience of life as you observe it in your outer and inner worlds.

Sigmund Freud, the psychologist who created and developed psychoanalysis, believed the mind comprises three distinct parts: the conscious, the preconscious, and the unconscious. According to Freud, your conscious mind is everything you are aware of. Your preconscious mind is the part of you with emotions and thoughts that can become conscious when you pause and reflect. Finally, there's your unconscious mind, which contains all the memories and desires you can't consciously think of or access.

Ask a scientist what consciousness is, and they'll tell you it's a product of the brain. From a scientific perspective, it's impossible to be conscious or aware without a living, functioning brain that has every neuron doing its job. Francis Crick and Christof Koch are two brilliant neuroscientists who claim the neural networks in that amazing organ in your skull are responsible for giving you the ability to know you exist in the world around you - and to process your inner experiences as well. Yet, scientists haven't cracked the code of the neurobiological mechanisms that lead to consciousness. It's still a mystery - at least, according to scientists who don't subscribe to quantum ideas or the paranormal.

Now, what about quantum physics, also called *quantum mechanics*? This form of physics is focused on understanding phenomena you can only observe on the smallest of scales. It's all about how molecules, atoms, and subatomic particles work and interact. Look at life through the quantum lens, and you'll find all sorts of strange things that don't line up with regular classical physics!

According to classical physics, when you throw a ball up in the air, it must land, right? You've likely seen this happen countless times. In quantum physics, the ball might disappear, then pop back into existence, change colors at a speed faster than light, and then land - *probably*. That's because there are more possibilities besides the ball simply landing.

What's the connection between consciousness and quantum mechanics? Experts in this field claim consciousness is the result of activity that takes place on the quantum level. Multiple theories on the quantum mechanical production of consciousness exist, collectively called Quantum Mind Theories. You didn't pick this book up to learn the ins and outs of quantum mechanics in detail, but it helps to know some of the major points in this field that are connected to consciousness.

**Wave Function Collapse:** In quantum physics, the universe is an ocean full of endless possibilities that are all happening simultaneously. This concept is the *wave function*. In the world as you know it, when you toss a coin, it's either going to be heads or tails. In the quantum world, it's both heads and tails at the same time. This state is called superposition, but the moment you look at the coin, you cause a wave function collapse, forcing it to be either heads or tails.

This suggests your consciousness or mind is the cause of the wave function collapse. Your observation, part of your consciousness, causes you to experience life as you do. If you'd like to experience something else, you have to turn your attention away from the current reality to a different one out of the endless possibilities available.

**Quantum Brain Mechanics:** Think of each brain cell as part of an orchestra. Each neuron has a different role to play, but it works along with all the others to create a beautiful piece of music, which is, in this context, your consciousness. Physicists understand that this symphony is the result of quantum processes.

Experts suggest that the microtubules in the brain cells cause consciousness. The microtubules of the neurons are in a superposition, similar to the coin that's both heads and. This is the concept of quantum brain dynamics.

**Entanglement:** Pretend you're holding two dice in one hand. When you roll them, each one will stop on whatever number it does, and neither is controlled or influenced by the other. Yet, in quantum physics, these dice are entangled, which means no matter how far apart they are from each other, the result you get after rolling one will immediately affect another. This strange quantum magic is called entanglement. This isn't a mere theory. It's already been observed and confirmed by these brilliant quantum scientists.

The connection between the concept of entanglement and consciousness should be obvious. Whatever you are conscious of - whatever your thoughts and emotions are - is reflected in your reality. Wake up thinking it's going to be a bad day, and watch how hard life works to give you things to complain about. Entanglement suggests that your consciousness has a deep connection with reality as you experience it.

## Higher Consciousness

If consciousness is seeing a tree, higher consciousness is seeing the tree, the entire forest, and then some. It is awareness on steroids. It's perceiving things beyond your ordinary consciousness's capacity to pick up. This form of consciousness isn't just about knowing where you are, who you are, and how you feel. It transcends your subjective experience of life and connects with something more significant, or, as some would put it, the divine or universal consciousness.

When you connect with higher consciousness, you are connected to a state of awareness that is beyond yourself. It's a state beyond your limited ego, which is why it's also called expanded consciousness. Some think of it as a part of the brain that people have access to now and then, and not for long each time. You could consider it the opposite of your primal desires and instincts.

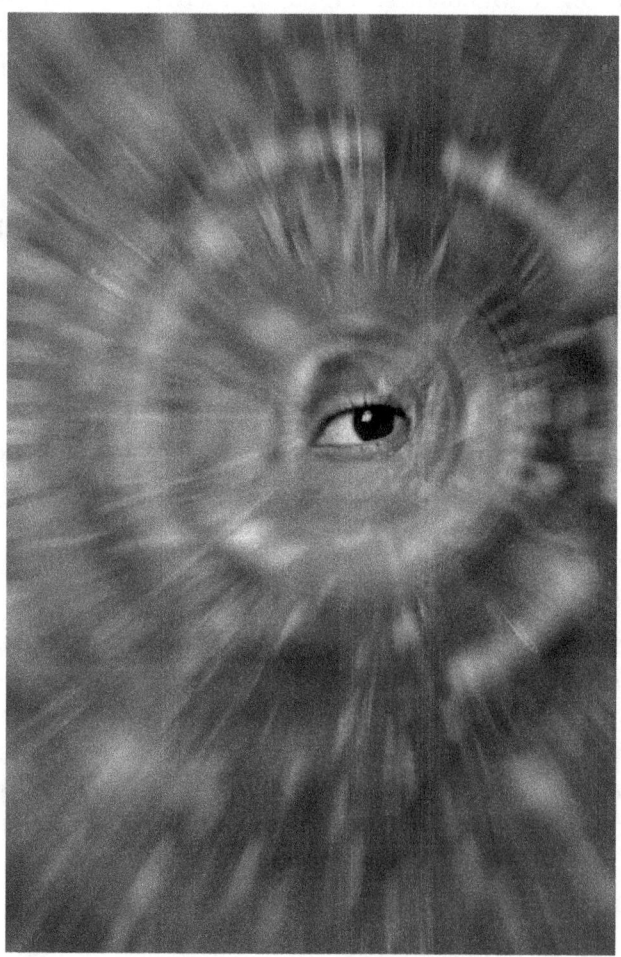

**Higher consciousness is perceiving things beyond your ordinary consciousness's capacity to pick up.**[80]

Most people live their lives in lower consciousness, which is also known as the ego. The ego isn't a bad thing because it has its function. After all, there's no way to live in this modern world without it, but the trick lies in knowing that it's not you. It's a costume, and like all costumes, it can be changed. Identifying as your ego means you shut yourself out of the world of possibilities available to you.

Your ego is the sum of everything you think you are, your assumptions about yourself and others. The most self-involved people function from the ego alone. When you tap into higher consciousness, you're less selfish and more self-aware. Your heart is full of compassion and empathy, and it feels natural to be kind. Every decision you make using higher consciousness is rooted in love rather than fear.

Why does higher consciousness matter? What use is it to you? If your spiritual development is important to you, then it would serve you to learn more about higher consciousness and how to tap into it every day. On the surface, it seems like there's nothing more important than having a job, paying your rent, staying up to date with the news and new technology, etc.

Achieving success, having a high status in society, and increasing the number of zeros in your bank account seem so crucial in today's world, but most people are missing one truth. Success in all its forms can only come to you if you're willing to develop yourself. True self-development begins from within. It starts with you becoming aware of your spiritual self.

Fulfillment comes from feeding your soul with everything it needs to express itself more fully through your life every day. Everything in the physical world is the result of spiritual action. You can't take enough physical action to get the feeling of satisfaction that every human instinctively desires and reaches for – unless you learn how to live from the perspective of higher consciousness. Doing this, you are *"tuned in, tapped in, and turned on,"* as Abraham, channeled by Esther Hicks, says.

If you find yourself feeling dissatisfied with life lately, it could be because you are finally waking up to the fact that there are more important things than promotions, possessions, fame, and status. You could be at the top of the pyramid, rubbing shoulders with the crème de la crème, and still feel empty if your soul is starving for a connection to divinity.

Some think that once they reach higher consciousness, nothing bad will ever happen, and there will be smooth seas and clear skies in the scheme of things from that point on. You start receiving inspirational ideas that lead you to where you need to go when you act on them. Your perception of yourself is clearer as you become more aware of yourself and the reality of life.

This increase in awareness is never-ending. There is no final destination where you "retire" from spiritual work and enjoy the benefits indefinitely. There's an ebb and flow, times where you're more tapped in than others.

It's like being a professional soccer player. You know how to pass, shoot, and dribble. No denying that you're good on the field, but that doesn't mean you never make mistakes. Sometimes, you make a pass, but an opponent intercepts the ball. Sometimes, you try a sliding tackle, but you miss and wind up with a yellow card.

In the same way, there will be times you forget to stay connected to your higher consciousness. When this happens, you regress to being who you were before you began your conscious spiritual journey, living from the mindsets of fear and limitation. You don't have to be afraid of this, though, because when you fall, you can always get back up and keep going.

## Methods of Attaining Higher Consciousness

Humanity has used various methods to attain higher consciousness for hundreds of years. Monks, shamans, and yogis are some of those who have always known how to set their egos aside and connect with the infinite intelligence of the higher mind.

Fortunately, you won't have to sequester yourself away in some monastery or remote region to tap into the spiritual reality of life. The methods used to get to this state of awareness are accessible to you here and now. Here is a quick look at some of them.

**Meditation and Mindfulness:** Meditation is deliberately focusing your attention on one thing. Your point of focus could be an object like a candle's flame or a spot on the wall. You may prefer to focus on your breathing or count a specific sequence of numbers. You can keep your attention on a mantra, a short word or phrase that carries a spiritual energy you'll experience the more you focus on it. By focusing on one thing only, you become a master at directing your attention. With practice, you'll be calmer and more stable, regardless of what you're experiencing in life.

Another form of meditation is mindfulness. This practice is about becoming conscious of yourself and every moment. You learn to be aware of what your mind is up to by noticing your thoughts without judgment.

You pay attention to what you experience on the inside and the outside through your five senses. You notice every desire and feeling that arises within you, neither judging nor identifying with it. If you're always anxious about your future or regretful about your past, you'll find mindfulness a useful practice because it grounds you in the present.

**Contemplation:** When you take time to think deeply and reflect on something, you are contemplating it. Think of it as a form of meditation, except this time, you're focusing on an idea, a question, or even a verse from a sacred, spiritual text. There are no limits to the subjects you can contemplate. You could reflect deeply on the nature of reality, what the solution to a problem would look like, your life's purpose, the person you have been versus who you'd like to become, etc.

Contemplation is not the same thing as thinking in the usual sense. It has nothing to do with planning your day or being concerned about what tomorrow will be like. All you do when you contemplate is allow your mind to settle on that question or idea you want to focus on. You trust that whatever you need to know as you contemplate this thing will blossom in your mind. It's not about trying to figure it out on your own. Instead, you're keeping your mind open and giving yourself space to allow information related to the subject you're contemplating to come up within you.

**Fasting:** Before anything else, if you decide to take the fasting route to higher consciousness, please check with your medical health professional first to ensure there is nothing to be worried about. You know what they say - *better safe than sorry.*

Fasting is a spiritual practice that has existed for thousands of years and is still practiced worldwide today. Most people in Western society are quick to condemn anyone who practices fasting. Part of that reasoning is the result of capitalism, which has sold people ideas like "breakfast is the most important meal of the day" - just so a certain company can sell as many cereal boxes as possible!

When you fast, you abstain from food for a fixed period. You could also abstain from drinking anything (that would be a *dry fast*). A fast can be as short as a few hours or as long as weeks. By fasting, you purify your body and mind. In this pure state, it's easier to tap into higher consciousness and gain perspectives you'd never have if you were feasting as usual.

This practice helps you discipline your body and mind, reminding you that you are in control of these things and not the other way around. The clarity and inner peace you get from a fast help you remove spiritual or energetic blocks to experiencing higher consciousness in your life. Fasting brings you in touch with the subtle parts of yourself that you don't often think about.

**Chanting and Mantras:** When you chant, you repeat a specific word or phrase, and this brings you into the higher consciousness state. Chanting is an ancient spiritual practice, and the fact that people still do it today is a testament to how effective it is for tapping into higher consciousness. You could either chant aloud or silently in your mind. It's similar to meditation, except your point of focus is whatever you're chanting.

Mantras are sounds, words, or phrases you repeat as you meditate. You may assume it's the same thing as chanting, but there's a slight difference. Chanting is broader, as it's speaking or singing repetitively. You could chant a word, melody, or tone.

On the other hand, a mantra is a specific kind of chant. It is used in Buddhism, Hinduism, and a few other traditions. These mantras are usually short and have a profound spiritual effect on you when you use them. All mantras are chanted, but not every chant is a mantra. Regardless of what you choose, these tools will give you the divine connection you seek.

**Yoga:** Many assume yoga is only about physical poses and keeping fit. This practice has existed for thousands of years, originating in ancient India. Other than poses, yoga involves breathing techniques and meditation practices. Yoga is from the Sanskrit word yuj, meaning "to unite or yoke." This spiritual practice aims to achieve unity between your awareness and higher consciousness.

In yoga, the physical postures are called asanas. By practicing these postures, you prepare your body for meditation. As you flow from one posture to another, you quiet your mind. You become present, which is the best state for effective meditation.

By practicing these postures, you prepare your body for meditation.⁸¹

The breathing techniques are called pranayama. Yogis have always believed that the connection between your body and mind is in the breath – and they're not wrong. The next time you're in a fit of anger, slow your breath down. Make it long and deep, and notice how your mind relaxes.

Once you control your breath, you control your mind and the flow of energy in your body. When your body and mind are in the perfect state to connect with the spirit world, you can use any of the yoga techniques, including mantra meditation, concentration, and mindfulness. This is another path to higher consciousness.

**Entheogens:** In shamanic traditions, people – usually shamans – use entheogens to connect with higher consciousness. The word "entheogen" is from Greek, and it means "generating the divine within" or "generating God within." Also called sacraments, these are substances that induce an altered state of consciousness, allowing the shamans or the people they lead to connect to higher states of consciousness.

To be clear, this book is not encouraging or endorsing drug abuse. If this is an experience you'd like to have, it's best to go with a professional and get confirmation from your doctor that it's safe for you.

The cultures and traditions that use entheogens do not do so for fun. These tools are holy and sacred to them because they allow people to directly experience divinity. These substances rip off the veil of physical reality, allowing you to experience true reality, which is oneness, love, and light.

There are various kinds of entheogens, from synthesized versions like LSD to natural ones like psilocybin mushrooms and peyote. The peyote cactus has been used for spiritual purposes for more than 2,000 years in Mesoamerica. It's still popular among the Huichol Indians of Mexico. These sacraments give you insight and a broader view of life than anything you could imagine.

You're right to suspect there's some controversy around the use of sacraments, as some are concerned about the risks to physical and mental health when used in any other context than traditionally or with the help of experienced guides. For this reason, many of these substances are regulated or outlawed in most places. Regardless of the fearmongering, entheogens are undeniable gateways to higher consciousness.

**Ethical living:** When you choose to live according to ethics and principles like nonviolence, truthfulness, generosity, kindness, etc., you achieve the purity of mind that makes it easier to attain higher consciousness. You have a moral code and decide never to act outside of it.

It makes no sense to meditate every day, first thing in the morning, only to harm others by being dishonest and cruel or deliberately triggering people. There's a reason many spiritual traditions encourage living ethically in addition to other practices for connecting with divinity.

Living by ethics requires self-awareness. Self-awareness makes you more conscious of other aspects of yourself connected with the Higher Mind. It's not just that you don't hurt people, but you also take every chance you get to cultivate positivity. You care about other people's well-being and yours. This is why Buddhism proposes the Five Moral Precepts:

- Respect for life
- Generosity
- Responsible relationships
- Truthful communication
- Mindfulness

When you live according to these ethics, you keep your mind pure and reduce the noise that drowns out the voice of spirit within you. Your awareness expands, helping you attain higher consciousness. If you're about to take action and unsure if you've made the right decision, think about whether that choice aligns with your spiritual goals, and you'll have your answer.

## How Higher Consciousness Changes Your Life

*"I experience peace every day - even when I shouldn't."*

*"I used to be the most anxious person I knew. I can't believe once upon a time, I thought that was something to be proud of. I thought it meant I thought of everything so I'd never be caught off guard. Over the years, that anxiety became such a burden that I couldn't function. Panic attacks became the norm for me. I had a nagging feeling that I needed to take up meditation, but I had no idea how to do it in the first place. After doing my homework, I began to meditate every day for 10 minutes.*

*"The effects of my daily meditation practice began subtly at first. Something happened at work, and one of my coworkers pointed out that they were surprised I didn't panic as usual. After that day, I began paying closer attention to myself. I noticed the space between my triggers and the reactions that followed. In the past, I would have reacted without thinking. Now, thanks to my connection with higher consciousness, I'm more aware of my emotions. I can feel them without letting them steal my peace - no matter if I'm having a good day or a bad one."* - Jane

*"I fell in love with myself.*

*"For a long time, I never liked myself. That's putting it mildly because I loathed who I was. I did a good job covering that up by acting confident, sometimes to the point of arrogance. But I was filled with shame and guilt for years. I thought that was life and everyone felt the same. It was only after a conversation with a trusted friend that I realized I had a problem. As heavy as the burden I carried was, it was good to know that there were other ways to be besides how I'd been living.*

*I started going to therapy, where I discovered the past trauma I'd gone through and what limiting beliefs I had that affected every part of my life since I was a child. I realized the person that I'd been all this time wasn't really who I was. I was a living trauma response. When I started doing spiritual practices alongside my therapy, this was when my healing reached* new levels. One of the most profound experiences for me was connecting with higher consciousness through meditation and contemplation. I had an amazing session where I was suddenly overwhelmed with a feeling that I didn't have a word for. If there's a word for 'the greatest love ever,' that would be it because four letters don't describe what I felt that day.

"I felt reborn. I felt awake for the first time in my life. I felt this greatest love flowing through my body, overwhelming my mind to the point of its nonexistence and bursting out of my being. If I had anticipated this, I'd have taken a moment to mourn my former self. The old Jared that got me to that point had died that day.

"Later, I learned that this was the "ego death" experience. It was more than the realization that I didn't have to be the person I'd always been. More than that, I couldn't relate to my old self anymore. I now understand that I have one purpose in life, and that is to love everything, everyone, and, just as importantly, myself. Not for anything I stand to gain, but just because." - Jared

These are just two stories about how your connection with higher consciousness can radically transform your life for the better. Here are more ways that your connection with Divinity will affect you:

1. Your energy becomes softer as you release anger, aggression, and pain. This leads you to have a better attitude about your life.
2. You'll be more in touch with your intuition and learn to follow it without question.
3. You'll drop bad habits and pick up new, better ones. You may have new hobbies or interests and meet new people who line up with your energy. You may even switch careers, preferring something simpler and less demanding.
4. You'll reduce your materialism. This happens because you recognize there are more important things in life than money and stuff.
5. You accept responsibility for your life, knowing that you are where you are because of you and nothing else. You no longer play the blame game - even with yourself. Holding yourself accountable doesn't mean bashing yourself for past bad decisions. It's knowing if you got yourself into something, you could get yourself out of it. It's taking action.

6. You no longer expect people and things to make you happy because as you attain higher consciousness, you recognize that happiness is an inside job. You also stop defining yourself as a success or a failure based on what the world says or your old limiting beliefs.
7. You experience more miracles and synchronistic events. Everything about life is synchronicity, but when you attain higher consciousness, this synchronicity becomes clear as day. You recognize that you are in a never-ending dance with infinite intelligence. You've always been, but you didn't realize it until you woke up.

Higher consciousness allows you to do so much for yourself and others. Do you feel lost and confused? Would you like the most reliable guidance about how to handle a situation? Is there a problem you've been trying to solve that's proven difficult to crack? Do you need physical, emotional, or mental healing? No matter what you need help with, you will get your answers once you connect with a higher consciousness.

You'll know that you've attained this altered state of being when you experience it. There will be no doubt in your mind. This is the same state that shamans enter to work in the spiritual world. Higher consciousness is the origin of intuition, which is inner teaching and knowing that is beyond whatever your rational mind can come up with. You can experience this in lucid dreams, where you are awake and conscious within your dream, exploring the worlds within. This is the same as Christ-consciousness and God-consciousness, a state full of wisdom, love, and understanding. It is the Buddhist Nirvana where you are set free from the illusions of this physical world.

The vastness of the universe is beyond comprehension. It continues to expand outward and inward into infinity. You are an intricate part of the universe. There is no disconnection between you. You are entangled, as the quantum physicists say. So, if you want to know more about yourself, you should learn as much as you can about the universe. Where do you begin? Find out in the next chapter.

# Chapter 2: The Quantum Cosmos

*"As above, so below. As within, so without. As the Universe, so the soul."*
- Hermes Trismegistus, The Kybalion

Now that you have a solid understanding of what higher consciousness means and you're familiar with the bit of quantum mechanics, it's time to take a look at the universe itself. There's so much to ponder about the universe. How exactly did it come into existence? If The Big Bang led to the creation of the universe, then what caused The Big Bang? If something or someone caused The Big Bang, who or where are they? They have to be somewhere, which would mean there is more than one universe, right? Did their universe begin with a Big Bang too? If it did, what or who caused their version of the Big Bang? Just how many Big Bangs ar there? Is the entirety of existence done Big-Banging around, or still at it?

If The Big Bang led to the creation of the universe, then what caused The Big Bang?[245]

There are still more questions to consider. If the world is still expanding, what is the point of it all? What part are you supposed to play in this vast cosmos? You may think that God has all the answers, but that raises a new set of questions. Who is God? Where is God? Who or what is the source of existence itself? What's the deal with all the deities across cultures, traditions, and religions?

Turn your attention to outer space, and you'll find even more questions burning within you. If time passes differently within a black hole, what is the true nature of time? Is it real? What makes reality real?

If you're going to ask questions about time, you may also question its counterpart, space. What is space? Is it real? What does it mean if you are a fractal of the universe? If every part of the universe is reflected in your being, does that mean you're a universe? Would that imply that all space between things doesn't exist? If you're a universe, are there Big Bangs happening inside of the inside of your inside, ad nauseam?

This chapter will help you understand everything about your place in the universe. You'll develop an expanded awareness of life. It's essential to finish this chapter before moving on to the next because it's the key to unlocking a deeper understanding of the subjects discussed in the chapters to come.

## The Birth of the Universe

Where did the universe come from? Many theories seek to answer this question, but one of the most accepted ones all over the world is The Big Bang theory. This theory says the universe began from one atom that existed before time itself and then rapidly expanded in a cataclysm of cosmic proportions. According to Big Bang theorists, the universe started from a compact size. How compact, you wonder? The answer is about a million billion billionth of the size of one atom.

The energy of this primordial atom was denser than anything imaginable. Its density was so great that it combined electromagnetism, gravity, and the strong and weak nuclear forces, creating a single one. Over time, as matter cooled down from the bang, more particles formed. More time passed, and these particles became the stars and galaxies you know.

You can't talk about the universe without discussing dark matter and energy. These two things are still mysterious, but there's no doubt they are responsible for the creation of the cosmos. Dark matter is a different kind of matter. It never interacts with light, which means there's no way to see it. The only reason you know it exists is because of the gravitational effects it has on galaxies and galaxy clusters. It's like Gorilla glue on a cosmic level, as this dark matter keeps all the galaxies together where they need to be.

The Big Bang left behind a soup of particles that continue to expand and cool down, all thanks to dark matter.

On the other hand, you have *dark energy*. This particular kind of energy is in all space and is why the universe continues expanding faster. The intriguing thing about dark energy and dark matter is they are 95% of the universe. The remaining 5% is all the regular matter that you see every day. That should make you wonder what's going on with the 95%.

At least five billion years ago, the rate of acceleration of the universe's expansion picked up speed. After much research, scientists have concluded that it must be dark energy causing this acceleration. While they're still at a loss as to the true nature of dark energy, the effects of this energy are undeniable. It's a force that increases the space between galaxies, which leads to the ultimate expansion of the universe.

There's a delicate balance between dark matter and dark energy. Dark matter helps to keep things together through gravity, while dark energy pushes things apart, which causes the expansion of the universe. You could say these two phenomena are the architects of the history and the future of the universe. Scientists believe the more they understand these mysterious twin forces, the better they can tell where the universe is going and how to prepare for that destination.

## Multiple Universes?

The multiverse theory suggests that there are many other universes besides this one. This is something phenomenal to ponder because the universe you're in is already vast. It's full of hundreds of billions of galaxies. How many stars are in your universe? They are beyond counting. It's even more mind-boggling to realize that the stars and galaxies exist throughout 10s of billions of light years. In other words, take 9.4607, multiply that by 10 to the power of 12, and you get almost 6,000,000 million miles.

Now multiply that figure by 10s of billions, and it's immediately evident that one universe alone is a lot. So, the thought that there may be other universes besides this one is both amazing and terrifying. There might be many versions of you out there doing exactly what you're doing, and many more being versions of yourself that you could never imagine, doing things that have never crossed your mind.

The multiverse theory also suggests that each of these universes could have entirely different laws of physics by which they operate. There could also be other life forms that you aren't familiar with. As your body is a universe of individual cells, life could be a collection of universes - a multiverse. This is a theory that is debated in philosophy and physics.

One of the most prominent depictions of the multiverse is rooted in inflation theory. According to this theory, an event occurred when the universe was in its infancy - the briefest period since it came into existence. This infinitesimally short amount of time was when the universe began its rapid expansion, or inflation, to become incomprehensibly larger than its size before the inflation.

Experts claim the universe you're in stopped its inflation 14 billion years ago, but the fascinating thing is, just because the inflation has ended with this universe does not mean it's ended everywhere else. So, right now, multiple universes are still experiencing inflation. This universe is simply one of many universes that pinch from much larger ones still in the expansion process. The process is eternal, creating more and more singular universes.

The theory that life is eternally inflating means each universe should have its laws and particles. Each one has forces that it respects. The constants of each universe are also different from here on Earth, and that's why it's nearly impossible to explain dark matter with regular classical physics.

Is there any validity in the idea that there is a multiverse? If you think about it, it's the fact that there is life at all. This universe has been specially orchestrated to allow intelligent life forms to exist that can observe the cosmos. It seems as though some intelligent force has set things up deliberately to support life.

Think about how abundant carbon is. Consider the importance of light for photosynthesis, which allows plants to grow and sustain all other living beings. How convenient is it that a big ball of light is up in the sky, helping plants grow and thrive? All of these things together couldn't possibly be a coincidence. The existence of life, as you know it, suggests an intelligence responsible for creating it.

Certain versions of the multiverse theory suggest every decision you make causes a new universe to be created. This is where you have the concept of parallel realities. Are you starting to realize how expansive and intricate all of life is?

## Your Soul's Role in the Vast Cosmos

If all of life continues to expand and there are many versions of you, the question to ask is, what is your purpose in life? What role is your soul supposed to play in this cosmos? It may almost appear that all of it is meaningless if you attempt to answer those questions through the lens of the limited human paradigm, which assumes things gain more value if they are scarce and vice versa. That's certainly one way to think about it.

Think about the fact that the whole is the sum of its parts. You are part of the universe, which means you have a part to play. You are inherently relevant and of great value. Without you, the world would not be as it is. Your perspective and ability to observe the world is an intricate part of the existence of life. The finite and infinite may seem separate, but they are one.

Imagine you're a drop of the ocean. At first, you may assume that you are irrelevant compared to this huge body of water. From your limited perspective, it's clear why you'd think this way. Now imagine every other drop in the ocean thinks the same way that you do. Each one decides to go its own way. What would be left of the ocean? Nothing.

You are performing your soul's sole purpose by being yourself.[88]

Your soul has its part to play. This truth echoes across various cultures, traditions, and faiths, demonstrating how essential you are to life. The light of creation shines through your unique state of being, experiences, and interpretations of said experiences. You express the power of divinity, whether you see it as the omniscient Abrahamic God, the impersonal Hinduist Brahman, or that which connects one and all as in Taoism. Whatever labels you use to express this divine essence, the point is that it exists, and simply by being yourself here and now, you are performing your soul's sole purpose: to reflect and express the Source of all life.

The idea of multiple universes may not exist in every spiritual tradition, but reincarnation is an interesting parallel. Reincarnation is when a single consciousness or soul explores different lives in the same universe. Since the multiverse theory suggests there's more than one universe, your soul can experience itself within more than one reality, facing unique challenges and different goals in each one. You are a part of the whole, doing your part for the evolution of consciousness.

This idea is synonymous with the beliefs held in tradition, similar to Sufism. You contain the perfection of the divine source of all things, and your life itself is the process of revealing this perfection. It's the same idea as the Buddha nature, where the goal is to become enlightened, or in the Hindu understanding of the True Self, also called the Atman. Before creation, all things were one thing. For this one thing to know itself fully, it had to create another. As a result, the one thing has become what it is and what it is not – which is also part of what it is.

In simple English, you are the Source of all life, understanding itself through your perspective and experience of itself as "not-Source." How do you know what cold water is if you've never touched hot water? How do you know North if there is no South? How do you know who you are without also knowing who you aren't? Therefore, your soul's ultimate purpose is the grand revelation of the Creator.

If you've always wondered where God, deities, and other beings fit into the ever-expanding puzzle of existence, the answer must have become apparent to you by now. There are many names to describe this one force that created and still creates all things. Many stories attempt to capture the essence of this same thing, which is less a thing and more like a being that embodies infinite intelligence and all of existence. Regardless of religion or tradition, they all attempt to capture the same thing: the story of the Creator of the universe, still in the process of creating.

As there is an omniscient God, there are other beings that are emanations of God, "less than" the Creator in the sense that they, too, have been created. In the Kabbalah, they're called the Sefirot, emanations of Ein Sof, the infinite Unknowable God. These emanations are the different aspects of divinity responsible for guiding humanity to ultimate enlightenment.

Think of these as the angels, guides, and other beings who are said to guide humanity's spiritual evolution and help them navigate the maze of life on Earth with increasing grace and wisdom. Whatever name you assign it, there's a single Source from which all deities and other lesser divine beings spring.

Across spiritual traditions, you'll find guides, teachers, and deities playing critical roles that all assist the human soul on its journey to enlightenment, which is unity with the Source of all life. These beings have enough experience, having traveled much further along their evolution. From their evolved state, they reach out to the travelers coming behind them. They're here to say to you, as in the book of Isaiah, chapter 30, verse 21, "...*This is the way, walk ye in it...*"

Deities, guides, ascended masters, angels, and other similar entities share the knowledge they gleaned from when they were where humanity is presently in their respective journeys. These beings benevolently guide everyone back home to their true self. They have embodied higher consciousness in ways that humanity is yet to achieve, so their guidance is a helpful gift.

As for the Source they (and you) come from, it lacks personality – not because it's boring, but because it contains all personalities itself by being the space and power behind the creation and evolution of galaxies and the life forms each one carries. Whether it's the idea of a creator or deities and other beings, you must wonder about the observer effect and its implications.

According to this quantum physics tenet, by observing something, you affect the way it behaves. This begs the question, is humanity in some way influencing the existence of these deities and beings? Are people simply interpreting formless energy and consciousness through the lens of these traditional and spiritual beliefs, creating real experiences of these beings and their abilities?

Are the people who meet and connect with these beings, whether in real life, dreams, or visions, simply summoning them through the power of their belief? Also, when you have more than enough people believing in the same thing, surely that should be enough to create an entire universe of spiritual beings, shouldn't it? If the observer effect is true - and it is - does that imply you, too, are a creator? There are no right or wrong answers per se. These questions are simply interesting to ponder.

If you've studied spiritualism, you know there must be a spirit world. This world exists beyond the physical. It's a world where things you'd consider impossible are possible. In this space, you'd expect to see ancestral spirits, guides, and other beings you may not ever have read, heard, or thought about. People connect with these beings either on their own or with the assistance of genuine psychics and mediums. You, too, have received messages from the spiritual world if you've noticed synchronicity, those meaningful coincidences that force you to pause and be here, now.

With this fresh perspective, your interaction and connection with your God or other deity should evolve. You now understand that you weren't meant to accomplish your soul's mission in a bubble. There is an entire team that would be happy to assist you, at least according to spiritualism and religious beliefs. Even if you consider yourself an atheist, it's nice to know that there is an infinite neutral force you can rally to your goals. Whether you call it willpower, focus, determination, or attention, it's all one and the same energy. It's a higher consciousness.

## Time, Reality, Fractals

When you think about time, chances are you consider it linear. You think of the past, the present, and the future. Quantum physics doesn't view time in that way. Instead, time is interconnected. The past, present, and future do not flow sequentially.

If you close your eyes and try to replicate the events of yesterday at 4:00 PM, you would be in that time right now. If you imagine a possible future for tomorrow at 5:00 PM, you would be in one of many parallel realities where that is exactly what took place right now. Everything is here and now. There is neither before nor after. You only perceive it that way because of the physics of this world. On a quantum level, it's all happening right now.

Even spiritual traditions have interesting things to say about this. Your past, present, and future all exist, whether you perceive them right now or not. This idea of time is the principle behind such manifestation methods, such as using your imagination to go back in time and change what happened so it lines up with the present or future you'd rather experience.

**What makes reality real?** From everything you now know, you can infer that there is an ultimate reality. You can also infer that there are subjective forms of reality. There are as many realities as there are people. Even if there's someone in the room with you right now, you are both experiencing two completely different versions of reality.

This becomes even more complex when you consider what's happening in your inner world versus theirs. While you may be sitting in front of a laptop trying to figure out the next words to write in a chapter of your great novel, they may be on vacation somewhere in the Cayman Islands, sipping on a Mai Tai in their imagination.

Some suggest that any reality that cannot be observed by people other than yourself is not real. That's a rather reductive way to think of reality. If you wanted to go along with their argument, what would they say about people who experience shared visions and dreams? Some have a more generous definition of reality, claiming that if you cannot perceive it, it isn't real. This definition does away with the need for other observers in the room.

However, if this were true, what about all those times you were stuck in an anxiety dream, for instance? When you're in the middle of dreaming, the world around you feels real, but when you awaken, you no longer have access to that world. You cannot perceive it unless you go back to bed and pick up where you left off in that dream.

So, according to the proponents of the second definition of reality, your dream world went from being real to unreal, and that's not logical.

The truth is there are many layers to reality. There's the physical world you pick up on with your five senses, but that's only one of many realms. The physical world is the product of a much deeper reality made of pure consciousness. It is the source of all things and beings, as well as events that have happened, are happening, and will happen. This resonates with the spiritual concept of the Akashic records, a spiritual storehouse of all experiences and kinds of knowledge in existences known and unknown.

Things get even more interesting when you consider the quantum physics side of things, where the observer effect suggests that reality is pliable. If you can mold it to fit your preferences and expectations, in much the same way you control what happens in a lucid dream, the question becomes this: *Are you awake, are you dreaming, or is it all the same thing so it doesn't matter anyway?*

It is said that every person is a fractal of the universe. A fractal is a pattern that repeats itself in the whole of a thing as well as its parts. Think of the Fibonacci sequence, for instance, which shows up in all sorts of objects, from flowers to buildings. Your soul is a fractal of the source of all things.

The fact that everything in life is fractal is what makes it possible for you to find analogies in nature to explain your life experiences. It is why if you strip different systems down to their core, whether religious, financial, political, industrial, or otherwise, you can find similar patterns repeating themselves in terms of how these systems run and how those who operate within them behave.

This sentiment of being a fractal of the universe demonstrates that there is no separation between you and everything else in life. The web of divinity connects one and all, whether you are conscious of it or not. This is not to say there is no relevance to your unique individual perspectives and experiences, but that you are part of a grander whole.

This chapter has one purpose: to blast your mind wide open regarding these concepts and have only one perspective of time, the one you perceive. As a result, it is nearly impossible to access higher consciousness and change your life radically. You've been taught that reality is fixed and relentlessly continues as it is through time unless and until someone with great vision changes things. With this chapter, you now know what Louise Hay meant by her quote, "*The point of power is in the present.*" You don't have to settle for things when you can make them as you prefer.

You've also been taught to view yourself as separate from everyone else. Once you question this idea you've been spoon-fed all your life, you'll realize that part of the blocks you experience in your attempts to create the life you prefer is this idea of being apart from everything and everyone else. This belief is a wall that keeps you from what you should receive.

Think of it like this. If you are yourself and the person who has something you need, why would you not give yourself what you seek? You already have it. Knowing you're one and the same as others who seem different is one of the keys to receiving your desires in the physical world. The moment you become conscious of the truth that you are everyone, and as Neville Goddard put it, "*everyone is you pushed out,*" you will experience miracles like never before.

# Visualization Exercise – Connecting with the Universe's Energy

Don't be intimidated by the word "visualization." It's the same as imagination. The following is an exercise to help you get in touch with the feeling of connection between yourself and the universe. You'll get the most out of this visualization exercise if you do it somewhere free from distractions.

If you live with other people, please ask them to give you at least 10 to 15 minutes with no disturbance. If you have any devices with you, it's best to leave them outside the space or turn them off so you're not distracted by notifications, alarms, or phone calls. Ensure you're wearing comfortable clothing that allows you to breathe and move freely, and check the room's temperature so it's not uncomfortably hot or cold.

1. Sit or lie down in a comfortable position. Close your eyes.
2. Pay attention to your breathing. Notice the inhales and exhales. With time, each will naturally become deeper and longer. When you feel a sense of presence or stillness within you, you're ready for the next step.
3. Pretend you're floating gently off whatever you're resting on. Feel what it would be like to have gravity release you as you float higher and higher.
4. Imagine floating up through your roof and into the sky. Watch the clouds pass you by as you head higher and higher.
5. Now you're in space, a dark backdrop with many twinkling stars as far as your imaginary eyes can see. Feel the sense of wonder fill your heart and soul as you realize you're looking at the universe.
6. Now, look down at your whole body, from your chest to your feet. Notice your body emitting a soft glow that gradually shines brighter. Feel your body, heart, and soul becoming one with this light. Know that you, too, are now a star.
7. In your star form, imagine you can see glowing threads of energy in the form of light, connecting you to all the stars and planets around you, as well as every life form in the universe.
8. Notice energy flowing back and forth between you and everything else. You're connected to it all.

9. Feel your ego dissolve as you lose your sense of self and become one with everything. Feel the power, peace, connection, and wholeness permeating all of you to the point where you become the whole.
10. Remain in this state for as long as you desire or until your timer alerts you.
11. When you're ready to return, take a few conscious, gentle breaths. Give your toes and fingers a wiggle to become aware of your body once more. Then, after counting down slowly from five to one, open your eyes.

You've just felt the raw power of the connection you have with the Universe or, if you prefer, with the Source of life. Do this exercise each day, and watch how radically your mind and life are transformed for the better.

Now you know about the true nature of reality and time, how the universe came to be, what your soul's mission is, and what God and the other divine beings have to do with it all, it's time to learn about the vast treasure house you carry within you in the next chapter.

# Chapter 3: Tap into Your Inner Power

*"Knowing others is intelligence; knowing yourself is true wisdom. Mastering others is strength; mastering yourself is true power."* - Lao Tzu, Tao Te Ching

For a long time, humanity has been preoccupied with discovering what lies in the ocean's depths or the vastness of space. Another important place needs to be explored as deeply as possible but is often neglected. This place is the vast world within you. So, in this chapter, you'll take a deep dive within yourself and explore terrain you never knew existed.

What's the point in being a know-it-all if you know

"Knowing yourself is true wisdom."[84].

everything except who you are? What's the point in gathering all this information only to let it go to waste because you're not using it? This chapter will be very practical, so if you intend to make the most of it, set aside whatever you're doing and give it your full attention. Otherwise, you may want to pick a different time when you can give this your full attention and practice what you'll learn here.

## Why You Should "Know Thyself"

Why should you take time to know yourself? If the story of your life is feeling lost, confused, helpless, and hopeless, then knowing the power you carry within is the first step to setting yourself free from a life full of experiences that do not fulfill you.

There's not one person on the planet who doesn't feel the call to explore themselves. Everyone has a latent instinctive understanding that true power lies within, but this terrifies so many that they'd rather look for substitutes than the real thing.

So, they observe how other people who embody their inner power behave and attempt to copy that. Rather than adopt the state of being, they mimic it. Some try to make up for their lack of awareness of this power and how to wield it by going after power, money, and sensual pleasures. Sooner or later, they realize that those things must pale compared to the treasures within. If you can relate to this, then be glad you have been led to this book, this chapter, and this very moment.

You cannot solve the complex problems of life by imitating others without the energy that fuels their behavior and gives them their results. You won't find any satisfaction in seeking external validation either. True power comes from a place of authenticity, and you can't be authentic if you don't know who you are or what you're here for.

You have to deliberately look inside yourself to get to know the beautiful, the ugly, and the in-betweens, accepting them as the perfection of your being. The knowledge you have of yourself will be your compass, guiding you towards your True North to a fulfilling life that leaves an impact for the better.

If you choose to mimic others, you come from a place of inauthenticity. You're admitting that you don't have the power within you. You'll feel disconnected from your life and have a profound sense of emptiness that won't let you go. Copying others means putting on masks, makeup, and costumes, which can be very heavy and ill-fitting.

You did not incarnate into this existence to be a replica of another person in terms of self-expression and creativity. Everyone is an individual. You must find what makes you truly you and then express that. If you prefer to be a professional mimic, you not only concede your power to others but also limit your potential. That's not what you want.

True power comes from a place of authenticity.[85]

You want the clarity that comes with knowing your inner power. When you know what your values are and where your passions lie, these things are a beacon calling you toward the next step of your enlightenment. You proceed toward your dreams and goals confidently because you trust in the power you carry within. Your authenticity is undeniable and attractive to others who are like you.

## Quantum Principles and Becoming Aware of Yourself

All things in the world are interconnected, and you're a part of it all. Would you believe a grain of sand in your hand holds the entire blueprint for existence? Well, as illogical as that might seem, it does, and so do you. As you've already learned, in the quantum world, particles exist in multiple states simultaneously. They have an effect on one another regardless of their distance, and they're also affected by an observer whose presence causes a change in their states by wave function collapse.

On the surface, it may seem none of these things have anything to do with your personal journey or becoming more self-aware, but that's not the case. Consider superposition and the infinite sea of possibilities available to you. Just as a particle exists in more than one state at the same time, so are you full of a myriad of possibilities within.

There's a cosmic buffet of options available to you, with every item yours for the taking. The key to expressing a specific version of yourself, therefore, is to turn your attention to it. As the observer of this different version of your life, you cause a wave function collapse that allows you to break past your limiting beliefs about what's possible for you and express yourself as this new, more expansive being.

What about quantum entanglement and what it says about everything being interconnected, no matter how far apart? This is an excellent metaphor for the connection you share with the world around you and the people in it. Recognize that you and everyone else are part of a collective or a body. If you cut your toe on a sharp rock, it needs to heal. Would you not dress the wound to help it? Would you say, "My toe isn't me, so that's none of my business?" Of course not.

If you have a need or something you want to manifest, and you rely on others to make decisions that will bring you the desired results, here's what you need to understand: you and those people are interconnected. When you trust that they, as extensions of yourself, will fulfill your need, it's as good as done. Even if you find this hard to believe, your interactions with others will reflect your expectations. They will either meet your needs or confirm your doubts by not fulfilling them. In essence, you receive what you observe and assume to be true about others.

Your desires reflect your authentic self. They represent who you are. If you haven't done the work to figure out what you are about, what makes you tick, what makes your heart sing, and what is absolute drudgery, then you're full of everyone else's ideas but yours. You live a life led by the world outside of you, pulled this way and that, tossed and turned by the tides and currents of the ocean of life.

The problem is that the observer effect is always in action, which means if you continue giving your attention and energy to the things that don't represent your ideals or higher self, you'll get more of the same. The life of an unconscious creator is full of chaos and turmoil. You don't have to keep suffering that. By learning who you are, you develop a stronger awareness of your thoughts, beliefs, and feelings. Self-awareness gives you more control of your inner power, allowing you to take the rudder of your life and steer your ship where you want it to go.

## Energy, Quanta, and Inner Power

It's time to talk about the threads that connect energy, quanta, and your inner power so you have the essential knowledge to help you connect with and express more of a higher consciousness in your daily life.

The universe is a collection of various kinds of energy. "Quanta" is a word that defines the building blocks that make up the universe. They are little packages of energy, waves, and ripples of the universal ocean of energies. It's easy to confuse the quanta for energy, which is a more generic term, but they're not really the same. Quanta refers to tiny packages of specific kinds of energy, such as matter or light.

Now, what is it that drives the feelings you have? What's the source of your thoughts and actions? It's your inner power. This power is an expression of universal energy which is found in everyone and everything in existence. It is the spark of divinity that spiritual traditions and religions speak of. With this understanding of your inner power, the question is, what's the connection between energy quanta and the power within you?

Remember, separation does not exist. That you can see space between you and another person does not mean that you are not intricately connected. You share a connection not just with other people but with life forms and your environment, whether it's natural or man-made. You are made of the same energy that expresses itself in many forms, *whether as a rock, a cat, or a light bulb!* This is a quantum mechanics concept. Experts in the field have proven time and time again that everything in the universe is nonlocal. This principle of nonlocality implies that regardless of how far away you perceive something or someone from yourself, you are still connected.

What's the connection between this and your ability to work with your inner power to manifest your desires and develop a more conscious connection with higher consciousness? Assume you have an old-school radio set. If you want to listen to a specific radio station, you have to turn the dial so it matches the frequency of that station. In the same way, when you align the energy within you to match your desire's frequency and the infinite storehouse of the universal energy, you lock in on the manifestation of your desire. Stay with that frequency, and soon, more and more things in your life will shift or change to match it.

It all begins by becoming aware of your beliefs, emotions, and thoughts. Many live assuming they have no say about how they feel or what they think, burdened by the lie that the mind is in charge of them. They don't realize the mind is a tool they can use.

Imagine a carpenter who says, *"I don't use my hammer. It uses me."* Unless what you want them to fix isn't that serious, you have deep enough pockets, and you're curious about what they meant by that absurd statement, you wouldn't hire them.

So, *use your tools.*

Your ability to feel, think, and act are tools. Your mind is a tool, not your master. If you doubt that, the next time you have a negative thought, put it on a proverbial stand and grill it with questions about its validity, presenting any and all evidence you can come up with to prove it isn't true. You'll be surprised at how quickly you'll dispose of that thought when you've finished.

Do this exercise with any longstanding beliefs, too. If you think those will be a little difficult to disprove, remember what a belief really is; a thought you've been thinking for long enough and often enough that you think it's true because it resonates with you. In other words, you've thought it long enough that you, your life experience, and the thought are now an energetic match.

To tune your dial to the frequency of your desires, you deliberately select thoughts and feelings that match them. It may not feel natural at first, but if you do it long enough, it will become a habit. From then on, you'll act in line with those new feelings and thoughts, and this will lead to tangible changes in your life that encourage you to keep going.

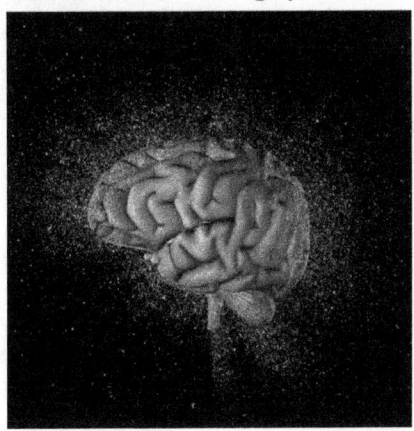

**You control your mind, not the other way around.**[36]

As you evolve, you'll grow more aware of your thoughts, beliefs, and feelings. Keep your focus on your desires. Set a clear intention, and remind yourself of it as often as you can so you resonate with it. With time, this resonance will be obvious in your daily experience. Remember your unity with the universal energy in all this, and you'll see great results. The following are practical exercises to help you connect with the infinite power within you.

## Practical Exercises to Tap into Your Inner Power

### The Seed of Awareness Meditation

1. Find somewhere quiet and comfortable.
2. Sit upright, keeping your back straight, elongating your spine as if there's a rope connected to the top of your head, pulling you skyward.
3. Begin breathing deeply, taking your time with your inhales and exhaling until your lungs are empty. Keep your attention on what your breath feels like as it enters and leaves your body.
4. While you meditate, thoughts will come to your mind and distract you from your breathing. This is completely natural. Acknowledge them when they arise, and don't judge them or identify with them.
5. Once you recognize that you have been distracted, feel gratitude that you noticed, and then turn your attention back to your breath. Do this as often as you are distracted, and never beat yourself up about it.
6. Sit in silent awareness of your breath for the next 10 to 15 minutes.

Use this simple meditation as a starting point for other practices that require going within. You'll have more powerful results this way than if you jump into other advanced meditations or visualization exercises like the next one. It works because it's like shutting the door on the physical world to become more conscious and aware of the spiritual realms within you.

### Visualizing the World Within

1. Begin with your eyes closed. Become aware of your breath, like in the previous exercise. When you feel present and still, it's time to visualize.
2. In your imagination, imagine walking down a beautiful pathway toward the entrance of a magnificent garden. Notice the way your

feet feel as you walk to the garden.

3. Enter the garden, and then stop just inside it. What do you see, hear, and smell? Pay attention to each of these things your senses pick up on, taking your time to study them. Maybe there's a babbling brook with gentle water sounds that put you at peace, an exquisite-looking bird flitting around, or an enchanting flower that draws you in.

4. Now, go further into the garden. Explore it, and notice the way you feel as you do. This garden is a reflection of your inner world. Note what it looks like, whether dreary and abandoned or flourishing and radiant.

5. As you explore, ask yourself what needs to change in your life to help you develop spiritually and become more of the person you'd like to be. If you haven't received an answer yet, don't worry. You'll receive it another time, probably when you're in the middle of something mundane.

6. If your garden looks like it needs some love, you can touch the plants and imagine light flowing out of your palms to heal them.

7. Spend 5 to 10 minutes enjoying your garden's sights, sounds, and smells or tending to the parts that need love.

**Firing Up an Energy Ball**

1. After getting yourself into a meditative state, rub both palms together briskly for a few seconds until you feel the heat and tingle in them.

2. Now, pull your hands apart gradually until there are a few inches between them.

3. Pay attention to the feelings between them. It's a subtle energy.

4. In your mind's eye, imagine there's the energy between your palms as an actual ball of light.

5. Play with this energy by bringing your palms closer together and pulling them further apart than the first time. Feel the energy ball grow bigger and less subtle as you do this.

6. Now, imagine that as you keep bringing your palms together and apart, the energy becomes more intense each time.

7. Imagine changing the color of your energy ball, and then pay attention to the feelings that come up as you do this.

8. Now, bring your desired intention to mind. Keep your focus on your intention, and notice whether the ball's color and energetic feeling change to reflect your desire. Note that you must focus on this intention or desire as if it's already done, with a heart of gratitude.
9. Keep this energy ball between your hands for some minutes, soaking in its energy and enjoying the feeling.
10. When you are ready, bring the ball up to your face. With a deep, long breath, imagine you're inhaling the energy ball. Feel it go in through your nostrils, filling up your chest and then spreading its radiance through the rest of your body.
11. Now, see your body glowing inside and out with the light from this energy, pulsing brighter and brighter.
12. Offer thanks. You can keep it short and sweet with a simple "thank you" or spend more time being thankful for everything about your already fulfilled desire.

**Seeing Auras**

An aura is the energetic essence of a being, showing their current state of mind or general "energetic attitude." You can use auras to tell if there's something wrong with someone and they need help or if they mean you harm. For this exercise, you'll need a room that's not too bright but not poorly lit either. You also need someone else to help you here.

1. First, get into your meditative state.
2. When you feel centered, open your eyes and gaze at a solitary object in the room. Keep your gaze soft. You're not trying to penetrate it. Stare hard, and you'll strain your eyes and get no results.
3. When you've spent a few minutes staring at the object, slowly move your attention to the person whose aura you'll be seeing. Use your peripheral vision. Looking directly at them will keep you from seeing their aura.
4. Wait patiently. Initially, what you see may only be subtle, but with time and consistent practice, you'll see their aura with ease.

**Discovering Your Power Animal**

Your power animal is one of those beings assigned to you to help you through life. You can draw wisdom, guidance, knowledge, strength, and power from them. The following is a great exercise to help you learn who they are and connect with them from here on out. After meeting them, if you need their help with anything, you can also use this technique to revisit them and make your request. Here's how it works.

1. Once you've attained your centered, meditative state, imagine you're moving down into the Earth's core, passing by tree roots and rocks.
2. Imagine emerging from the Earth into the most beautiful, natural landscape you've ever seen.
3. While here, ask your power animal to reveal themselves to you, and thank them in advance for answering your call. Wait patiently, with a heart full of thanks and excitement.
4. When they appear, thank them for revealing themselves and for helping you navigate the ups and downs of your life. Ask for a deeper connection with them, and thank them once more.
5. When you're ready, imagine moving up into the sky, reencountering rocks and tree roots – and then emerging back into your body in your room.

These exercises aren't the only ones you can use to connect with higher consciousness and channel your inner power wherever you desire. There are many more out there if you do your research. Also, suppose you feel intuitively led to tweak these exercises or create your own. In that case, you should trust that hunch and develop your exercises.

You'll get the best results if you practice them daily, even if you can only afford five minutes each time. Consistency is the key to success here. If you don't get immediate results, or nothing happens the first few tries, that doesn't mean you've failed. Don't pressure yourself with expectations.

Instead, keep an open mind and keep up the practices. Think of them like brushing your teeth – you'll do that every day, whether or not you feel like it. Now you've learned how to "go within," you'll discover how to "go without."

# Chapter 4: Go Beyond to Expand Your Awareness

*"Whatever you come across, go beyond."* - Nisargadatta Maharaj

You've learned to explore the worlds within you, but there's more to explore. Do you know you can travel from your body to worlds invisible to your physical eyes? Some of these worlds mimic the physical world closely, while others are so fantastical that it's difficult to imagine them if you've never been.

Astral projection and shamanic journeys are not the same.[87]

People confuse astral projection and shamanic journeys, thinking they're the same thing when they aren't. The only similarity they share is they're both metaphysical practices meant to put you in contact with worlds beyond the physical realm. In this chapter, you'll learn how to use them for spiritual exploration and connect with higher consciousness on a deeper level.

## Shamanic Journeying

For many centuries, shamans have used shamanic journeying to explore all the realms of consciousness that are unavailable to the physical senses. On a shamanic journey, you can communicate with spiritual beings such as your power animals, spirit guides, and other entities.

On this journey, you are in a state of consciousness where you can receive information from various levels of reality. Sometimes, while the shaman travels, their body is temporarily inhabited by the spirits of benevolent beings who impart much-needed healing and information to those who need it.

Prepare your mental state before embarking on a journey. You need to have a clear reason for wanting to visit these other realms, so spend time setting your intention for each trip. It's also best to practice this in a space where you feel safe and secure. If you feel fear, you may attract low vibration, unwanted entities, and energies to you, which would disrupt your session.

There are several shamanic techniques you could use to get into a state of trance that allows you to connect with different levels of consciousness. If you struggle with a journey, you can enlist the help of your spirit guides, power animals, or other beings you believe in.

## Benefits of Shamanic Journeying

Apart from how interesting it is to experience worlds other than your own, there are numerous benefits of practicing shamanic journeying.

. One of the most remarkable ways to draw on your inner power for healing is by using shamanic journeys. On your journey, you'll encounter guides who are knowledgeable in the healing arts and can diagnose the precise problems you're struggling with. They have experience beyond time that extends across all realms and will know what to recommend.

Sometimes, they'll act directly on your issue by sending healing energy into whatever part of your body requires it. The healing you receive from these beings is so profound that it also cleanses you of whatever negative, low vibrational energies led to your condition in the first place.

Here's a disclaimer. *You should see your medical doctor first whenever you have physical health issues or talk to a counselor or therapist if you're struggling mentally.* If you're still struggling to get better, then try shamanic journeying. You see, every problem in the physical world has a spiritual origin. There's no better way to address health issues than by working with higher consciousness in conjunction with the conventional help you receive from licensed, professional doctors and therapists.

**Your Stress Level Will Decrease:** Something about this metaphysical practice leaves practitioners feeling relaxed and at ease when they return to the physical world. They travel to other worlds full of peace and serenity and soak up the energy there. When you return from a trip, the reminder of the vastness of the cosmos makes your worries and concerns seem infinitesimally insignificant. The more you practice shamanic journeying, the easier it is for you to put life in perspective.

**You'll Discover Who You Really Are:** Many people today become what they've been told they should be rather than be their true selves. This is one of several reasons that people are mostly miserable. When you go on a shamanic journey, you will meet yourself – without all the frills and trimmings the world has put upon you. You'll learn much more about yourself than you could ever conceive through contemplation.

Some of the things you discover may seem unsettling at first, but keep an open mind. Self-discovery is always worth the time and energy. Once you learn more about your power, you can't go back to living a life weighed down by others' expectations about how you should behave. You know what's right for you and what isn't, and you are unfazed by any external pressure to get you to be something other than who you are.

**You Solve the Most Difficult Problems You've Struggled with Your Whole Life:** Is there a particular issue that has left you stumped for a long time? You think you've come up with the perfect solution, only to find that it all falls apart when you apply it. This failure has happened repeatedly, to the point where you've become disillusioned and are ready to give up. If you can relate to this, you should definitely try shamanic journeying.

With shamanic journeys, you can reach out to your personal guides and ask them to let you know where you're going wrong. They'll point out what you've been missing. They'll help you make the energy change to bring about the manifestation of the solution to this problem in a natural way.

**Your Creativity Will Soar:** On a shamanic journey, there is so much to explore, not just with what you feel and experience with your spiritual senses but also with your interpretation of those experiences. The vastness of the shamanic realms and how they express themselves is more than enough material from which to draw inspiration.

Regardless of your field of work, whether in the arts or some other industry not typically considered creative, you will find inspirational ideas to help you thrive. All you have to do is reach out to your guide and ask them to share what you need to know.

## The Three Realms

In shamanic traditions, the cosmos has split into three distinct realms:

- The Lower Realm
- The Middle Realm
- The Upper Realm

In some traditions, you'll find these three worlds are divided further into subworlds, but generally speaking, you encounter only three roads on your shamanic trance journey. You could travel to these worlds independently, but it's more usual to be accompanied by your spirit guide or power animal.

In shamanic traditions, the cosmos has split into three distinct realms."

**The Lower Realm:** Most travel to the lower world the first time they go on a shamanic journey. To get there, you'd have to descend into the earth using the World Tree, which is also called the Axis Mundi. This spiritual tree gives you access to all three worlds. You travel by moving through its trunk.

When making your way into the lower world, you have to go through a long corridor or tunnel, which you enter through the hole or opening in the earth. The hole could be one made by an animal, a waterfall opening, or a slit at the bottom of a tree trunk. It could also be a staircase that leads you down. However, the entrance to this world presents itself, and you will be entering the earth to get to the lower world.

The lower world is the realm of transformational power. In this world, your helper will be in the form of a power animal. However, other helpers could take the form of wind, trees, and other elements of nature. They could also be your ancestors, too. They'll appear in a way that resonates with you.

If you wish to enjoy your shamanic journeys, develop a relationship with these guides. The more time and effort you put into establishing a strong connection between you, the easier it will be to explore the shamanic realms and gain whatever you need from them.

The lower world is where you'll go if you need healing, transformation, and power in your life. The power you receive here will help you not only in your work but also in your spiritual development. This world is a representation of your inner psyche or subconscious mind. So, in a sense, it's not really about "going beyond" or "going without," but going within.

**The Middle Realm:** This middle world closely mirrors the earthly world but has everything to do with spiritual dimensions and the soul. Think of it like the earth as you know it but with an overlay of spiritual beings and structures. It's like pulling back the veil to see more of what's present in you that often goes undetected in the physical world. This is where you discover nature, creatures, and the different souls that make up nature itself, like the souls of pets, weather, trees, mountains, land, etc. It contains the present, past, and future of life on earth.

Is there something specific you'd like to know about some event? Do you want to gather information about a particular area? In that case, you should journey to the Middle Realm. From here, you can work alongside the soul of a specific place on earth or in nature. Every ritual practiced in different spiritual traditions and cultures involves drawing power from this world.

**The Upper World:** This is the world that sits above the Earth. You gain access to it by journeying into space and going beyond the stars. You can tell the difference between the upper and middle worlds by the difference in vibration if you're sensitive enough to pick up on it. The upper world vibrates at a distinctly different frequency from the lower one. This difference in vibration is also mirrored in the sort of assistance you can expect from either of these worlds.

For instance, if you want a higher perspective on your life and you want to find the space between yourself and a difficult situation that has overwhelmed you, you would be best served by going to the upper world. Also, if you'd like to discover new parts of yourself and ways to express your creativity, the upper world is where you should be.

You have two options when it comes to journeying to the Upper Realm. You could make your way higher and higher to the place beyond the stars through the Axis Mundi, or you could descend into the depths of the lower world and continue your descent until you emerge in the upper world itself. This is possible because these three realms are interconnected with one another. It's a cyclical route.

## How to Go on a Shamanic Journey

1. Get ready by finding a quiet space free from distractions and disturbances. You should feel safe and secure in this space.
2. Select your world. While nothing stops you from visiting the Lower Realm, seeing the Middle and Upper Realms may be more beneficial. If you're eventually led by your guides to visit the Lower Realm, then you can rely on them to get you there.
3. Decide what your intention is for this shamanic journey. Do you want healing? Do you seek clarity on a confusing matter? Would you simply like to get to know your guides? Whatever it is you want to do, get clear about it and fix it in your mind.
4. Begin drumming. If you don't have a drum, you can listen to shamanic drumming music for free on the Internet. If you find that too distracting, you can listen to your heartbeat. The point is to pay attention to a repetitive sound that is constant enough to cause you to enter a trance state.
5. Picture a great tree before you. This is the Axis Mundi that connects you to the different realms. Find the slit at the base of the tree and enter it, remembering to keep your destination

firmly in mind as you walk down the corridor toward the other side.

6. In the Middle Realm, explore the world around you with your intention in mind. You can also intend for your guide to show up and offer you whatever you seek or lead you to it. Don't be afraid to ask questions, engage with the entities you encounter, and observe the world around you.

7. If your intention is to reach the Upper Realm, find the Axis Mundi and climb it until you're up in the stars, and keep going until you're beyond them. Alternatively, ask your guide to take you there, and you'll both fly to that realm beyond the stars.

8. Once in the Upper Realm, remember to engage with guides, beings, and the world around you with your intention in mind.

9. To make your way back to the physical world, retrace your steps. As you emerge from the Axis Mundi, your awareness returns to your body in your safe space.

10. Take some time to breathe deeply, grounding yourself in your body by increasing your awareness of it. When you feel fully present, open your eyes.

11. Journal about your experiences, new perceptions you received, and any new questions that have sprung up that you can address on your next journey.

## Astral Projection

Astral projection is also called astral travel. When you go on this sort of journey, you're having an out-of-body experience or OOBE. Astral travel is a metaphysical process of transporting your consciousness out of your physical body and onto other planes of existence. Some say you're not moving your consciousness from your physical body to your astral one but only changing to your astral consciousness. However you want to describe it, you can astral project through visualization, meditation, lucid dreaming, and more.

When astral projecting, you'll notice all sorts of sensations from the moment you become aware that you are awake to when you actually leave your body. Astral projection will completely change the way you look at the world. When your astral body detaches from your physical one, you will realize that there is no end to life and no reason to be afraid of death when it comes.

Some people have the erroneous belief that astral projection is dangerous because it's possible never to be able to return to your body. Some say some other entity could possess your body while you're gone, but that's not true. Your body's yours, and no one has permission to eject you from it. Also, one of your main challenges will be staying out of your body as long as possible. Simply thinking about your body or feeling for it is enough to return you to the physical world, and there's a silver cord that keeps you tethered to your physical body.

If you want to succeed with this spiritual practice, it's better not to discuss it with skeptics until you've done it. No matter how stoic you are or how strong your will is, skepticism could be counterproductive to you making your first journey into the astral plane. Fear and doubt are the two most troublesome roadblocks to successfully projecting your consciousness from the physical realm to other planes, so do what you can to avoid them at all costs.

Here are some of the benefits of astral projection:

1. You can meet spiritual guides who'll offer insightful information about where you are in life.
2. You can use this realm to get inspiration for your projects in life. For instance, you could conjure up paintings, musical pieces, ideas for architecture, etc. The possibilities are endless.
3. In the astral realm, you can role-play what it would be like to live as the person you prefer to be. This will give you a clear picture of what it means to have manifested your dreams and make it easier and faster for those things to become physical.
4. You'll get rid of your fear of death once you practice leaving your body.
5. Astral projection causes you to become more self-aware, which is excellent for spiritual development.
6. Speaking of spiritual developments, the more you astral project, the more you'll experience anomalies in life that show you how plastic reality is, making it easier to create what you want in life.
7. You'll experience synchronicity and the awakening of various psychic abilities that you're unaware of or haven't been able to use to your fullest potential.

# How to Practice Astral Projection

**Get Your Mind and Body Ready:** If you want to project your consciousness to the astral plane successfully, you have to learn how to relax while simultaneously concentrating on your goal. Therefore, you should be in an environment that's safe, calm, and free from distractions. Meditating before your astral projection practice will give you better results.

You also have to release your fears. Astral projection is a practice that has existed for centuries and is perfectly safe. You won't lose access to your body because you're always tethered to it by a silver cord, which you may or may not see during your travels.

Before you begin, make sure you are in a comfortable position. Sit in an upright position or lie down. If you choose to lie down, beware that you may fall asleep before you successfully leave your body.

If you find sitting in an upright position uncomfortable, you could use a recliner or stack some pillows behind your back to imitate one. Make sure your body is clean and clear of drugs. Any depressants or stimulants could interfere with your goal and make it hard to leave your body - and that includes coffee and cigarettes.

**Close Your Eyes, Breathe Properly, and Relax:** You should take diaphragmatic breaths, meaning your stomach should rise with every inhale, and your lungs should be completely empty on your exhales. As you focus on your breath, you'll feel more relaxed. Try inhaling through your nose for four seconds, holding that breath for seven seconds, and then exhaling through your slightly parted lips for eight seconds.

**Wait for the Vibrations:** While you wait, resist the urge to move. Your mind will test you to see if you're awake because you're in such a relaxed state that it's as if you're asleep. It will send signals to your body to get you to turn over or scratch an itch. If you ignore these signals, your mind will assume that your body is asleep, putting you in a state of sleep paralysis, which is meant to prevent you from acting out your dreams.

In this state, you may begin to notice your body vibrating. It feels like intense currents of electricity flowing through you, but it's not painful. You can control the vibrations if you want by moving them around. Don't be surprised if you start noticing sounds like voices or laughter. It may also feel as if there are other presences with you in the room, but there is nothing to be afraid of. No matter what's happening around you, remember that you are safe. Don't be in a hurry to move to the next step. Take time to feel the vibrations.

**Imagine a Rope Above Your Head:** Keep your attention on this dangling rope for a while. Then, imagine reaching out of your physical body with your astral hands to grab onto the rope. Once the rope is firmly in your astral hands, pull on it to lift your astral body out of your physical one. You'll have a brief sensation of being in two bodies at once, so focus on using your astral senses rather than your physical ones. Continue pulling until you are fully out of your body.

**Move to the Furthest Section of Your Room:** From here, you can take a look at your body while sleeping in bed. Whatever you do, don't get excited or scared, as these intense emotions can yank you back into your body.

**Leave Your Room:** You could use the door if you wish, but being in your astral body means you can easily pass through solid materials. So, if you want to walk through walls to get to the outside of your house, you can do that. If you'd like to test what it's like to fly, gently tap the floor with a foot to bounce yourself into the air and then move through the ceiling up into the sky. With your mind alone, you can propel yourself in any direction at any speed you like.

**Explore Your Neighborhood, Town, Country, and Continent:** Since you're in your astral form, you don't need to adhere to the idea of taking time to move through space to get from one location to another. So, if you're in Cape Town, South Africa, and you'd like to be in Paris, you could get there by picturing or visualizing the Eiffel Tower or any other Parisian landmark that you know of. Even if you don't have a landmark in mind, the intention to be in Paris is enough to get you there instantly.

**Go Beyond the Earth's Orbit:** Nothing is keeping you from exploring beyond the Earth. To experience yourself as being truly connected to the universe, you should make your way into outer space, toward the stars and beyond them. You don't need to know what lies beyond to get there. Simply intend that this is where you'd like to go. You'll find the astral plane is very receptive and highly affected by your intentions, emotions, and expectations.

**Seek Your Spirit Guide and Ask Them Whatever You Desire:** Again, all you have to do is intend to meet with them. In the astral plane, you do not have to communicate with spoken words. You may use telepathy and receive blocks of thought that contain vast information from your guides.

**Return to Your Body:** To do this, simply think about your sleeping form on the bed or feel it, and you'll be there. Before you return, state firmly and aloud to yourself that you will remember everything you have experienced. This is a crucial step to downloading the information you've received instead of forgetting it once you wake up.

As you merge with your body, make a loud sound like a roar or a scream to help you connect your astral and physical consciousnesses. In this way, you are more likely to remember everything you learned on your journey.

Now that you know how to go within and go without, what's next? It's only logical that you meet your higher self, isn't it? Find out how to do just that in the next chapter.

# Chapter 5: Meet Your Higher Self

*"Sometimes your Higher Self will guide you to make mistakes so you can learn lessons."* – Gabrielle Bernstein

It's time to get to know your higher self. Once you do this, your life will be radically transformed. You'll wonder why you didn't look into this sooner than now, but better late than never, right?

Let yourself be your guide.[39]

# Your Higher Self

The idea of the higher self is familiar to many spiritual traditions. Some call it the I Am. Others call it the Authentic Self. You may call it the divine self, the mind, Christ consciousness, full potential self, fully realized self, universal consciousness, cosmic consciousness, soul, or self. Whatever title you choose, it represents a grander, greater aspect of you than you are currently embodying or capable of grasping right now.

As your higher self, you express love in its truest form. The love you share for yourself and others has nothing to do with ego. You could say your higher self is love itself. From the perspective of your divine self, you do not see any flaws in anything or anyone because you deem it all divinely perfect. This self never judges anything as evil and also does not acknowledge separation. Through these divine eyes, all things are emanations of the Creator. Your self is a beacon, a light that guides you back home to the unity of consciousness. It is infinite wisdom, love, and light.

It's possible to embody your higher self in your everyday life. Remember the quantum principle of superposition. As particles exist in multiple states, you can express your egoic self and hire yourself simultaneously for a richer, more rewarding life. What about entanglement? No matter how dark things may seem or how long it's been since you've given thought to the subject, your higher self will always be connected to you. If you're not aware of that connection, it's only because you have not put in the work to become conscious of it. This entanglement between you and the grander version of your being will make itself more evident when you deliberately reach out to connect to it.

By turning your attention towards your higher self, you activate the observer effect for good in your life. You cause your way of being to change for the better, to mirror this version of yourself that is perfection and love.

# Benefits of Connecting with Your Higher Self

What are the benefits you'll enjoy when you connect with your higher self and live with its consciousness daily?

**You'll Experience an Increase in Clarity:** By tuning in with this version of yourself, you'll no longer be bogged down by confusion or the feeling of being lost.

**Your Ability to Focus on What Matters Will Improve:** By keeping your awareness tethered to the cosmic and spiritual version of yourself, you'll find that you have no problems focusing on the things that matter the most.

**Embodying Your Higher Self Leads to More Mindfulness:** Mindfulness means being grounded in the present. You'll no longer be bogged down by what happened in the past or what may come in the future. From this perspective, you'll finally understand what Jesus Christ meant when he said in the book of Matthew, chapter 6, verse 34, *"Take therefore no thought for the morrow; for the morrow shall take thought for the things of itself. Sufficient for the day is its own trouble."*

**You'll Have More Respect and Compassion For Yourself:** Since your higher self is incapable of perceiving anything as imperfect or wrong, you, too, will emulate that quality. This compassion and respect will also extend to others in your life. You'll learn to value everyone, regardless of where they're at or what they're struggling with.

**Your Mental and Physical Health Will Improve:** Connecting with your higher self means allowing more of the natural creative energy that sustains the world to flow through you. If you constantly deal with depression and stress, you'll find this connection helps you feel better – in addition to therapy, of course.

# Cultural and Spiritual Perspectives on the Higher Self

There are many interpretations of the higher self across cultures and traditions. In the West, the higher self refers to you as a person but at your most spiritually evolved. You express uncommon wisdom, and your love is pure and unconditional compared to most. This statement is not an egoic thing, and there is no competition or pride. You are simply a being who resonates with these ideas. According to the Western perception of this idea, the true self is who you are when you are self-expressive and self-directed. As this person, you don't give in to the desires of the masses because you prefer to be independent.

Connecting to your higher self means shedding ego narratives about yourself.[40]

In Native American cultures, the people value being interdependent with one another, seeing that way of life as superior to the prevalent hyper-independence celebrated in modern times. So, their perspective on the higher self involves community. It is about honoring the threads that connect one and all in life. Therefore, in these cultures (and tribal ones), the higher self is the sum of these connections.

Spiritual traditions from the East view the higher self as your true essence. It's you with no limitations. As your higher self, you've surpassed egoic attachments. It's not separate from you but a key part of who you are that is still connected to the universal consciousness or infinite intelligence. To grow more connected to this self, shed all the layers of unnecessary things that the ego has piled upon your soul. In other words, strip yourself of everything you've assumed you are because they keep you from discovering your true essence.

## Stories About Connecting with Higher Self

*"My higher self loves to connect with me using synchronicities. Sometimes, she'll also speak to me with oracle or tarot cards. I remember this one time when I had a personal issue I was dealing with, and I cried a lot about it. Suddenly, I began seeing angel numbers popping up everywhere, and I'm very certain it was my trying to comfort me. The first time I met her during meditation, I was simply stunned by her beautiful energy.*

*She helps me out whenever I need to do work with crystals by choosing the correct ones for my needs. One thing she told me that I have taken to heart is that I shouldn't take life too seriously and instead, I should look at everything through a child's eyes."* - Fatima

*"I remember when I had begun meditating every day for 10 minutes. My desire to learn more about my spiritual life led me to discover a few videos on YouTube about how to connect with my higher self. One of the videos, in particular, called to me. I tried the exercise it suggested and left it at that. It took two months after four of my higher selves to make themselves fully known. When we established contact with each other, the feeling was intense. After that day, I noticed I pick up on their messages more clearly than ever."* - Vincent

*"Ever since I connected with my higher self, I have been experiencing miracle after miracle. Usually, these miracles start as seeming devastation or something to despair over, but things turn around for the better every time. My higher self has been teaching me that there's no reason to panic just because something bad appears to be happening. He has shown me that if I remain neutral or even positive in the face of these things, they will be transmuted into a better situation than before those events happened. The love I feel for the world and myself is so deep that sometimes I cry, especially in large crowds. The crazy part is that others cry along with me, like they know me and are glad to reconnect with me. I'm also experiencing telepathic communication."* - Zach

Do you feel inspired by these stories? There's no reason you can't have stories of your own. Take time to reflect on different moments in your life where you felt as if there was a higher power intervening or offering you guidance. For instance, was there a time when you felt strongly about something, and it turned out to be correct? That was your higher self in action. If you've ever felt intense peace and clarity even when things were not working out or appeared to be confusing, this is because your higher self fueled you with resilience.

What about your dreams? Are there any that stand out in particular? Do you recall meeting someone who felt like a teacher or a guide? Have you had any visions that revealed to you what you needed to do about a situation in your life? These messages come from your higher self as well.

Your higher self can use synchronicities of events and numbers to get your attention. Designed by freepik.[41]

Don't dismiss synchronicities. In the real sense of it, there's no such thing as a coincidence. Someone else may claim you're only noticing coincidences, but synchronicity is more than that, as a string of events plays out in a way that holds deep meaning for you. Your higher self can use synchronicities of events and numbers to get your attention.

## Higher Self Meditation

This excellent meditation will help you connect with your higher self. To perform this meditation, you'll need to tune into your third eye and crown chakras, which are energy centers that allow information and energy to flow into and out of your body and spirit. Your third eye chakra is on your forehead, slightly above and directly between both eyebrows, while your crown chakra is at the top of your head in the middle. Here are the instructions for this meditation.

1. Perform your basic meditation until you get to a serene state of mind.
2. Ground yourself by imagining roots that come out from the base of your spine and go down into the depths of the earth. Feel the stability and support these roots offer you.
3. Move your attention to your third eye chakra. Imagine an indigo light pulsing in this area. See it become brighter on each inhale, and as you exhale, imagine the light spreading through your body. Spend a few minutes doing this.

4. Now, move your attention to your crown chakra. Imagine a radiant white or violet light pulsing in this area. With each inhale, let the light grow brighter. With each breath, let the light flood your body inside and out.

5. Imagine a beam of white light that begins from your third eye chakra, moves up through your crown chakra, and towards the sky into the universe. This is the light that connects you to your higher self. Feel their energy flowing through you, full of love, wisdom, and guidance. Feel this energy flow in through your crown chakra and your third eye chakra and radiate through your body. Remain here as long as you like.

6. When you're done, imagine that the light beam from the sky gently retracts into your ground chakra and disappears. See the light in both chakras slowly dimming and returning to their regular state. After a few more deep breaths to ground yourself in your body, you may open your eyes slowly.

If you would like to connect with your higher self through shamanic journeying or astral projection, you can do this. All you need to do is be clear about your intention before you begin those practices, and when you are in that altered state or different realm, request their presence.

## 5 Tips for Connecting with Your Higher Self

1. Spend less time looking at screens and more time in nature or meditation.

2. Practice journaling daily to become more self-aware and track the different ways your higher self has made themselves known in your life.

3. Spend time contemplating your soul's purpose. If you've already worked it out, contemplate the different ways you could continue to pursue it.

4. Decide to trust your intuition with no questions asked. The more you trust it instead of leaning on your logic alone, the more accurate it will become with time.

5. Be consistent in all your spiritual practices. You'll have far more results if you do them every day than if you do them once every couple of weeks or months.

Now you know all there is to know about your higher self, it's time to discover how you can work with spirit guides.

# Chapter 6: Work with Spirit Guides

*"Your Spirit Guides and Angels will never let you down as you build a rapport with them. In the end, they may be the only ones who don't let you down."*

– Linda Deir

Spirit guides are divine entities assigned to guide and protect you throughout your life. You didn't arrive on the planet on your own. You know you have an entire team supporting and caring for you. They would do so much more for you if you would only acknowledge them and ask for their help because they respect free will and will not act unless asked.

Spirit guides can show up in the form of animals, among many other forms.⁴

Your spirit guides act as protectors, keeping you safe from dangerous situations. They are the best mentors who can guide you through the different issues of life, from business and finances to health and relationships, etc. This is because they have a strong connection to infinite intelligence and can offer you divine wisdom when you ask for it.

There's no limit to the forms that spirit guides can take to interact with you. It all depends on what your spiritual preconceptions and beliefs are, as well as the experiences you've had. Sometimes, they can show up as animals. At other times, they could be your angels, ancestors, or beings from other dimensions.

It should feel comforting to know that you always have a spiritual team at your disposal to help you remain conscious of higher consciousness and connected to your higher self. Your spirit guides are benevolent. There's no such thing as asking them for too much.

Where are these guides exactly? These beings dwell in realms that aren't physical. They operate through energy and vibration that's on the same frequency as the spirit world, which means if you desire to experience them more fully and connect with them daily, you should grow your spiritual muscles. Your daily practice with meditation, contemplation, and other spiritual practices will help you get to the point where you can easily connect with your spirit guides whenever you want without having to get into a meditative state.

Spirit guides play an essential role, acting as the bridge between the physical and the spiritual. If you struggle to progress in your spiritual journey by calling upon them for assistance, you'll be amazed at how much further you'll go. They'll help you discover the blocks in your life that keep you from accessing spiritual growth and dissolve them on your behalf, with your consent.

In other words, you don't have to settle for simply asking them what you need to change about yourself. You can also ask them for the energy and will to implement their suggestions, and you'll inexplicably drop habits that had always been hard to quit, picking up new ones that serve your highest good. Your spirit guides can help you discover your inner power and offer you information and knowledge that is not accessible to the ordinary person or obtainable through regular means.

If you've decided you'd consciously like to work with them, then you must build an attitude of trust and surrender. For too long, people have labored under the misguided notion that they must travel the journey of life on their own, and this makes things needlessly harder. Working with your spirit guides means letting go of this idea. Release your need to be in control. Slide over to the passenger seat and allow your guides to take the wheel. For best results, don't be a backseat driver.

If you need help to develop your intuition or improve your psychic abilities, your guides will help you. They'll help you become more sensitive to the subtle energies around you every day, and that can be very useful in navigating your daily life with others. So don't be afraid to ask them for their assistance and prepare for levels of awareness like nothing you've experienced.

## Types of Spirit Guides

**Animal Guides:** These guides are also known as animal spirits or power animals. Each one has a unique set of attributes depending on what animal they are since different animals symbolize different things. For instance, an eagle could represent vision, a bear could represent introspection and strength, and a butterfly could represent growth and transformation. Rather than rely only on generic interpretations of what each animal means, check in with your intuition. What does this animal represent to you? That's how you'll make the most of your connection to it.

**Ancestors:** Ancestors are the spirits of those connected to you by blood. The wisdom and guidance they offer you come from the collective experiences of their lives. Your ancestors are familiar with the challenges you face and the ones your bloodline, in particular, has struggled with.

Your ancestors could be people you've known from your past or those who passed on before you were born and had the chance to interact with them. For the most part, they have your best interests at heart, but if you choose to interact with them, you should specify that you only want to interact with those ancestors who truly care about your highest good. Why is this necessary? Well, imagine having Ted Bundy as an ancestor. Exactly.

**Ascended Masters:** These are highly evolved beings who have achieved enlightenment, having experienced multiple lifetimes – and learned so much from their travels. Jesus, Quan Yin, and Buddha are just a few of the most popular Ascended Masters. Not only have they had experience living on Earth, but they've also evolved on other spiritual dimensions. They've achieved unity with higher consciousness but choose to offer help and guidance to as many as call out to them.

**Angels:** Angels are celestial beings whose job is to guide you down the right path and keep you safe. There are various kinds of angels, but the most popular are the archangels. These are the angels who have specific qualities they're known for. For instance, Archangel Michael is typically called upon when one needs protection or strength. If you would like to be more creative and communicate better, then Archangel Gabriel is the best being to call upon. You can reach out to these beings or have them connect with you through your dreams, visions, and intuition.

Angels are spirit guides as well."

**Nature Spirits:** These spirits are responsible for the natural world. They have a profound connection with everything to do with nature and work hard to ensure all of life remains in perfect ecological balance. These are the spirits of the elements like fire, water, air, and earth – as well as of plants, rocks, mountains, etc.

This is by no means an exhaustive list of the different kinds of guides available to help you. If you need more information on who your guides are, you can always ask them, and they will tell you everything you need to know.

# How to Connect with Your Spirit Guides

There are multiple ways to connect with your spirit guides. If you've never had any supernatural experience before that would suggest that they exist, you don't have to wait for them to reach out to you first. You could be the one to initiate contact. These are the various ways to establish a rapport with your guides.

**Using Meditation:** You already know the basics of how to meditate. So, if you'd like to use meditation as a tool to connect you with your spirit guide, set an intention before you begin the process. Don't be dismayed if nothing happens after the first try. Continue your meditation practice with your intention front and center in your mind, and sooner or later, they'll make themselves known in the best way and at the best time.

**Through Dreams and Visions:** Dreams are an excellent way to establish contact with your spirit guides. For some, seeing physical manifestations of spiritual phenomena is a little too scary. Your dreams are the perfect setting for a meeting between you and your spirit guides. This is because you already expect strange things to happen in dreams, as a rule. So, it won't freak you out too much if certain beings approach you in a dream and let you know that they are your guides.

Do you want to connect with your guides through dreams? In that case, you should set the intention before you go to bed every night and also keep a journal beside you. As soon as you awaken from your dream, write down whatever it is they shared with you so you don't forget, and you can reflect upon the message later.

If you are clairvoyant or have some activity with your third eye chakra, you may also experience visions. Think of these visions as being similar to dreams, except they take place during your waking state. They could be as short as a quick flash or as long as your guides need to get their message across to you.

**Signs and Synchronicities:** Your spirit guides will send you specific signals, which could be in the form of notable events or unusual phenomena around you, to let you know that there's something more going on or that they are present. The signs could be patterns of events that repeat themselves, a gut feeling, or an intuitive nudge. The science could also come in the form of goosebumps, vibrations in your body, and a sudden sense of "knowing" the truth.

As for meaningful coincidences or synchronicities, they are excellent tools to help you become alert to the spirit world and the presence of your guides. Remember, when it comes to synchronistic events, their importance or significance lies in their meaning, not cause and effect. Synchronicity can play out in the form of angel numbers you see all around you. You could be thinking about your brother-in-law and suddenly get a call from him.

Maybe there's a big decision you have to make, and you're feeling confused about whether or not to act. Then you suddenly stumble upon a forgotten book on a bench, with a highlighted sentence on its open page that addresses exactly what you need to know.

Every time you receive these signs and synchronicities, pause and acknowledge them. Thank your guides for reaching out to you, and ask them to communicate with you in even clearer ways if you're feeling lost and confused about what they mean.

To maintain the flow of information between you and your spirit guides through signs and synchronicities, you should journal daily. Also, get into the habit of meditating whenever you notice these signs, especially if there is time and you have privacy. Set the intention to have these messages become clearer each time, and you will no longer question what they're trying to tell you.

**Automatic Writing and Channeling:** Your guides can communicate to you through automatic writing, which is a practice in which you get into a meditative state and then, prepared with your pen and paper or word processor, write down whatever flows through you without any thought. Channeling is the same as automatic writing, with the difference being that you speak your guides' messages rather than writing them down. Some of the most famous channelers known to the spiritual community are Esther Hicks, Darryl Anka, and Jane Roberts.

If you would like to practice automatic writing, get your writing tools prepared first. Next, set your intention to communicate with your spirit guides. Following that, begin your meditation, keeping your focus on your intention. When you feel still and centered, you can begin writing. Resist the temptation to try to understand what's flowing out of you. Even if the beginning appears nonsensical, trust that it will eventually have meaning, or the meaning will be revealed to you later when you review your notes.

If you choose to channel, you will do the same thing as with automatic writing. Prepare a recording app or device to record everything that you're going to say. Set your intention to communicate with your spirit guides, then enter into your meditative state. Once you're feeling centered, begin to speak as you are led. Once more, what comes through you doesn't have to make sense. The more you practice this, the better you get at picking up on the energetic impressions from your spirit guides and interpreting them accurately. You'll have less and less of your ego tainting their messages with its biases and assumptions.

**Divination:** Divination is a metaphysical practice that involves discovering what will happen in the future or discerning what's going on now or in the past. It is picking up on information that would be impossible to access through ordinary means. You can use several divination tools to connect with your spirit guide if that's your desire. You could use runes, tarot cards, pendulums, etc. Before using your chosen tool, use meditation to ground and center yourself, set your intention, and then begin your work.

You can use tarot cards to connect with your spirit guides."

Tarot cards come with pictures and text to let you know what each card means. You use them by shuffling them while thinking of the question you want to ask or asking it aloud. Then, you either keep shuffling until a card flies out of the deck, or you set the deck down and pick a card from wherever you're intuitively led. Apply the card's meaning to your question, and you'll have your answer. If it's not clear, ask aloud for clarification, shuffle the deck once more, and then select another card. This new card will offer more insight from your guides, clarifying the first answer.

Runes have their meanings, too. You only need to study what each implies, cast them, and read the answers from your guides. Pendulums are excellent for receiving yes or no answers to your questions, so consider studying how those work and investing in a good one for your practice.

# Tips to Facilitate Communication with Your Guides

1. Keep a journal of all the messages you've received and the questions you have for your guides.
2. Commit to trusting your intuition, and you'll get better at telling it apart from your regular thoughts and feelings daily.
3. Keep the space where you connect with your spirit guides sacred. If you can't for some reason, then whenever you're about to practice, you should envision a white light that clears out all negative, stale energies in the room before you start.
4. Learn to be patient. Learning to communicate with your spirit guide is not a one-day affair.
5. Ask them to give you signs and guide you whenever you can.

You know everything there is to know about how to connect with your spirit guides. Does the thought of exploring different timelines interest you? Would you like to know what you were up to in your past lives? Are you curious about any agreements or sole contracts you may have entered into that you're unaware of in this present life? The next chapter has definitely been written for you.

# Chapter 7: Timelines, Past Lives, and Soul Contracts

*"Stop wasting time! Time is growing short for you to accomplish what you came to Earth to do!"*

- Dolores Cannon, The Three Waves of Volunteers, and the New Earth

What's the point of exploring alternate timelines? Why do your past lives matter? Do soul contracts hold any water if you don't even remember them? Are they still binding? There are many benefits to learning about timelines, your possible past lives, and soul contracts that you may be a part of. By examining your past lives and any parallel or alternate timelines, you understand yourself better. You think you know your full strength, but there's always more to be discovered. The more you know about these topics, the easier it will be to pick up on the patterns in your life and identify ways to grow beyond your limitations.

By examining your past lives and any parallel or alternate timelines, you understand yourself better."

Like it or not, your present challenges are connected to other lives that you have lived and are living right now. When you understand what happened in your past lives, you will find the logical explanation for those seemingly insurmountable obstacles you've had to contend with in this life and resolve them. Armed with this newfound knowledge, you'll be able to heal yourself of past traumas, which will allow you to finally experience growth in areas where you've been stagnant for too long.

Knowing your origins is a great way to discover your sense of purpose. You'll know where you came from and where you're heading. It will become easier to work out if you are living according to your soul's true purpose or not.

Finally, considering everyone has a history beyond what is known in this present incarnation, it's easier for you to extend compassion toward them. You realize they're the sum of all the characters they've played across lifetimes, just like who you are is the result of who you've been.

## Do You Live Multiple Lives?

The first thing you must understand about existence is that time is an illusion. It may appear that you are living just one life, but you have more than one. According to Dolores Cannon, you are living many lives right now concurrently. Remember the idea of reincarnation? It is the spiritual concept that when you pass on, you return to Earth as a different person to learn new lessons or embody a new character.

If time is not linear and everything exists now, then that would suggest the idea of past lives is really the same as parallel lives. What people commonly refer to as "past lives" are parallel incarnations. So, as you read, note that both terms can be used interchangeably in this chapter.

**What people commonly refer to as "past lives" are parallel incarnations."**

You're just not aware of these other lives unless you peep in on yourself through past life regressions or dreams. Your consciousness is focused mostly here on your present incarnation on Earth, but that doesn't negate the existence of the other versions of you. Research Jane Roberts's work on the idea of the oversoul and its splinters so you can understand how this works.

As your body is made of multiple parts and organs, and each organ is made of multiple cells, you are one part out of an unfathomable number of lives, all connected to one soul. Put differently, if your oversoul is the ocean, your present awareness of this incarnation is one of the drops. You are one pinpoint of a grander, greater awareness than you currently have access to consciously. So, as you continue your spiritual evolution and your awareness expands, you begin to identify yourself in other individuals. The truth about your full self is that it is on God's plane where everything is united. There is no duality or separation. It is all one and the same consciousness.

How can you be certain that the idea of multiple timelines is a valid reality? The late Dolores Cannon did some amazing work in this field.

Working with hypnosis, she was able to help thousands of people with past life regressions. Throughout all these sessions, every participant gave her incredibly detailed narrations of their past lives across various cultures and epochs. Some of these people even spoke of past lives on other planets. The consistency of the results she got from her sessions indicates that there was no fabrication or fantasy involved. Why? Every story that was shared with Canon was later verified using historical research.

The people who worked with Dolores Cannon greatly benefited from the regression sessions. They found the connecting thread between what they experienced in their past or parallel lives and what they were facing in their present lives in terms of phobias, challenges, and gifts or talents that they inexplicably have. As these people revisited their past lives, they were able to resolve the trauma they experienced then. As a result, their present incarnation improved. They experienced profound healing and felt lighter and freer due to the emotional release from these sessions.

One interesting thing they all pointed out was their connection to the same set of souls across lifetimes, regardless of the setting or age. These souls changed roles from one lifetime to the next, switching from friends to family members and sometimes enemies. This raises the question, what is the point of these repeated dramas and reenactments of situations across reincarnations?

The whole point is the evolution of the soul. With each incarnation, whether you choose to call it a parallel life or a past life, you learn new important lessons that advance you to the next level of your spiritual development. As each person continues to develop towards their higher self, they contribute to the collective's growth.

Your soul is not bound by linear time. It experiences multiple realities simultaneously. It exists across multiple dimensions as well. When you die after playing your part in one incarnation, there is an in-between stage known as the *Life Review*. The stage is critical because it's where you go over the lessons that you have learned from the life you just left behind. It's where you experience your life through the eyes of everyone else with whom you've interacted with. You'll also get to connect with your loved ones from various lifetimes and plan what your next incarnation will be in this stage. The Life Review is not confined to the earthly concept of time.

Now you're probably wondering, how many reincarnations do you get? Dolores's work did not confirm any specific point at which you'll no longer have to incarnate. The reincarnation process does not end until your soul arrives at a point where it does not require physical experiences for its continuous expansion. When it gets to this point, it will not need to show up in this 3D universe. That doesn't mean the soul ceases to exist, but it goes on to other grander adventures that are beyond human comprehension. Your soul moves on to planes where it exists non-physically.

## By Will or By Force? All about Soul Contracts

Your soul made the deliberate choice to incarnate on Earth. Some say you are only kept bound to Earth by beings known as archons, who are the ones who pretend to be your loved ones waiting for you at the light at the end of the tunnel when you pass on. They say these archons are here to trap you into the wheel of reincarnation so that you are forever condemned to this 3D experience, and you should never go into the light.

According to the work carried out by Dolores Cannon, it's clear that you deliberately decided to reincarnate here. This does not happen by chance, nor is it some punishment or trickery. Your soul is eternal, and its goal or desire is to know itself. There's no better way to know yourself than to try on many different roles and see who you are in those shoes. The desire to know yourself is natural because it stems from Unity, the Divine Source.

Remember, in the beginning, there was nothing and no one other than the creator, who or which was All-That-Is. The only way All-That-Is could know itself was to experience duality instead of its default unity. Therefore, it created All-That-It-Is-Not. Your soul is part of All-That-It-Is-Not, ultimately All-That-Is, and where you came from. Since Source desires to know itself through you, you, too, seek to know yourself, and you do this through your incarnations and steady evolution.

Now it's time to talk about soul contracts. Making the conscious decision to reemerge in a new incarnation means entering into a sole contract. It's not a piece of paper. It's symbolic of an agreement that you have between your soul, soul groups, and spirit guides. This contract clearly outlines everything you intend to learn from the journey or next incarnation. This symbolic agreement contains every significant experience you are meant to encounter and the patterns that will repeat themselves in the form of karma so that you can resolve them in this new incarnation.

There's no reason to be terrified at the concept of a soul contract because it is a road map that lets you know what opportunities you have to grow and become an even grander version of the person you are. The word "contract" makes it seem you don't have any choice but to follow that particular blueprint, but there is much room for flexibility and innovation.

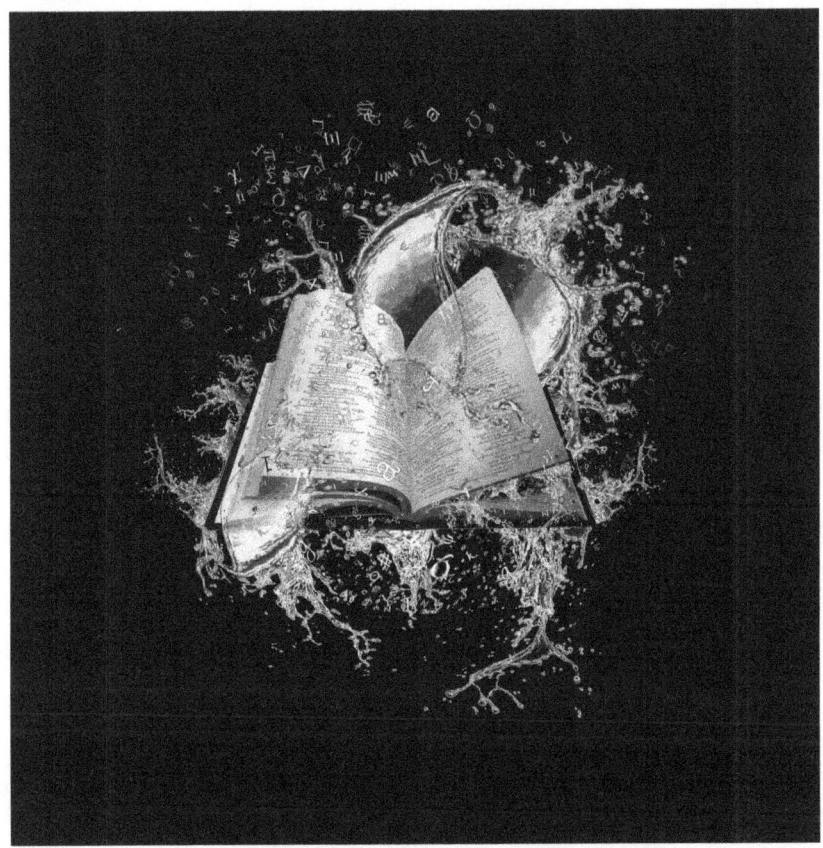

Per your soul contract, your soul chose to be on Earth."

Despite the existence of this agreement, you have free will. You get to decide what choices to make. You alone call the shots on how to navigate the challenges that present themselves to you. You decide whether to answer the call of divinity or ignore it. Clearly, you've chosen the former option because you are still reading this book. Every choice is critical to your soul's growth and will ultimately determine whether or not your contract will be fulfilled at the end of this incarnation.

A good question you may be asking yourself is why it's necessary to include challenges in this contract. Surely, there must be other ways to learn a lesson without difficulties and obstacles, right? You may find it beneficial to shift your attitude and perception of challenges. Every challenge and obstacle that you face in life is an opportunity for you to make decisions that help you grow. It's like going to the gym. The weights you lift are challenging, but you continue lifting them, and you become stronger with time. You'll be able to handle heavier things later on.

If you remember nothing else, realize your soul contract isn't set in stone. Depending on your experiences and the choices you must make, you could find extra lessons that were not part of the contract and may be inspired to renegotiate certain parts of that contract, working with your spirit guides and higher self who oversee the process. Remember, you are the observer. You always have free will, and the whole point of your existence is constant evolution from one incarnation to the next, even within individual incarnations.

## Case Studies

The best way to appreciate past life regression is through learning from actual stories and case studies of people who have explored the memories from other incarnations. From their stories, you'll discover how past lives continue to impact present ones.

**James Leininger:** James's story is an interesting one centered on a series of nightmares that began plaguing him at the tender age of two. Night after night, he dreamed about being in an airplane crash and the final moments before losing his life.

With time, James shared more details about his nightmares with his parents. What he shared with them left them horrified. Their son was convinced that he had been a pilot in another life. Unfortunately, his craft was shot down while he was in flight.

The level of detail James recalled led his parents to conclude that he must have been describing a real experience. Among many other details, he told them the name of the aircraft he'd been flying, the carrier, and the full name of one of his friends who had been in the service with him.

After doing some research, they discovered many parallels between what James had shared with them and the life of another James from a different time - James M. Huston Jr. This was a pilot who had served in World War II and had passed away decades before the present James was born.

**Two Hundred Children:** The former head of the psychiatry department at the University of Virginia School of Medicine, Ian Stevenson, MD, had thoroughly documented about 200 cases of children who had birthmarks that matched up with wounds that the people they believed they were in their past lives had suffered.

Ian cross-referenced the birthmarks on these children with the medical records of the people who had passed away that the children claimed to have been in their past lives. One of the children was a boy who remembered that he'd suffered a headshot. To add credibility to the boy's story, there were birthmarks on the front and back of his head, the points of entry and exit for the bullet that brought about his demise. Ian also came across a woman who claimed to have been struck three times with an ax before she passed on. Guess what she had? There were three lines on her back.

As Ian continued his research, he noticed that a great number of the children who remembered past lives had inexplicable birthmarks that could not be explained by any infections, genetics, or any logical causes. His findings revealed that 35% of these children were suffering phobias that matched whatever the circumstances of their past life deaths were. For instance, if one child remembered being thrown from a great height, the odds were that they now have a phobia of heights.

Another fascinating thing he discovered was that many of these children seemed to have a preference for clothing or food from specific cultures, which they claim they used to be part of in their former lives. His work provides overwhelming evidence that past lives are real.

**Jenny Cockell:** Ever since Jenny was a little girl, she began to experience vivid details of one of the lives she had lived in her past, early in the 1900s. She recalled being an Irishwoman who went by the name Mary Sutton. Not only did Jenny remember her personal experiences as Mary, but she also recalled those of Mary's children, to whom she still felt deeply connected.

Jenny became intrigued enough to go on a journey to find the people she once thought of as family in her past life as Mary. After a lot of time and research, she eventually traced her identity to Ireland. She was able to meet up with these people, and they confirmed that her memories weren't fantastical; they were accurate, down to the last detail.

# A Regression Technique to Connect with Your Past Life

So, you want to explore your past lives? Here's an excellent technique based on the work of Dolores Cannon. She came up with an interesting hypnosis method called the Quantum Healing Hypnosis Technique (QHHT), which is excellent for past-life regression, and the following technique is based on her work.

1. Get yourself into a relaxed meditative state using the meditation exercise you learned in an earlier chapter. You can sit or lie down. The choice is yours.
2. Once your body feels fully relaxed, imagine yourself in a peaceful place. Make it somewhere that resonates with you, whether a cabin in the woods, the beach, a forest, or wherever else. It should be somewhere you feel safe, secure, and calm.
3. From this safe place in your imagination, set your intention to explore whichever past life is most relevant to your present incarnation. You can call on your guides or higher self for assistance and tell them to show you what you need to see, which will be helpful for the evolution of your soul.
4. While in this space, allow your mind to travel. Don't try to control where your thoughts go. Allow feelings, impressions, and images to come to you freely. The scenes you see may show up in the space you have imagined, or you may be transported to a completely different place entirely. Don't have any expectations. Let things unfold however they will.
5. When you've finished, return your awareness to your physical body, take a few deep breaths to ground yourself, and then slowly open your eyes.
6. Write every thought in your journal as soon as possible to reflect on it later.

You now know how to check in on what's going on with your past or parallel lives. You understand the importance of doing this so that your present life can be more fulfilling and you can execute your soul contract flawlessly. So, what else is next? It's time to discover your higher purpose.

# Chapter 8: Your Higher Purpose Revealed

*"Focus not on what he or she does, but on keeping to your higher purpose. Your own purpose should seek harmony with nature itself. For this is the true road to freedom."*

– Epictetus

Now that you have a clear grasp of your soul's journey through consciousness and infinity and are acquainted with your guides and higher self, it's time to discover your higher purpose. Is this something that continues to elude you? Do you feel confused about the point of your existence on this planet?

It's time to find the meaning behind your existence.⁴⁸

You've worked out you are ultimately serving a goal of expansion, but the question is, what exactly are you supposed to be doing to make that happen? Where will you find the answer to that cosmic head-scratcher? This chapter will give you useful techniques to help you find a specific way you're meant to express your authentic self to live your purpose here on Earth.

## Why You Should Look Within

Discovering the ultimate purpose of your soul isn't something straightforward. While there are several modalities you can use to arrive at the truth of your existence, it's not something as easy as following a step-by-step guide. It would be nice if it were as easy as following the instructions on a frozen dinner, popping it into the microwave, and letting it heat up until it's time to take it out.

Your soul's purpose is not found in a book or a movie. The reason it's not so cut and dried is that your soul has wisdom beyond words and logic. It doesn't care what your mind thinks it desires.

In searching for your soul's purpose, you could talk to as many gurus as you like, read all the books out there, and listen to endless hours of podcasts, yet all of that work could never trump inner work. Your soul's purpose is in you, meaning there's nowhere else to look but within.

The problem with relying on an external source of information is you will only achieve superficial alignment. You're artificially assigning yourself something to be passionate about. If you dig deep, you'll realize this "purpose" isn't resonating with your authentic self. You may start with verve and enthusiasm, but eventually, you'll notice a growing sense of dissatisfaction and emptiness in your heart.

Defining your source purpose should never be left to external forces. You came here with your unique blueprint for how you're supposed to live your life. You will lose your agency if you look outside of yourself for the answers you seek. This is the reason many complain of feeling lost.

When you allow the world outside of you or your circumstances to dictate what you do with your life, you will live a life with no meaning. You didn't come here to conform. You came here to transform – and you can only do that by being your authentic self.

As you begin seeking your soul's purpose, you should have a sense of reverence. You have to stay open, trusting that whatever is revealed to you is for your highest good. You need the right frame of mind. If you're serious about knowing why you're here, you must cultivate a state of mind that is calm and clear. This means it's time to put away distractions like your favorite social media app. You also have to stop doing other things you know are getting in the way of finding your why. You know what they are. Your soul's telling you right now.

A final point to be made before diving into the different modalities of soul-purpose exploration is that the process is a journey. It's not something that's set in stone. At certain times in your life, your soul's purpose will evolve, and it is your job to stay in tune with it and keep up with its evolution.

## Soul Purpose Meditation

The world is full of stressed people. Stress is one of the reasons people find it difficult to discover their soul's purpose. Modern life is full of distractions and poor, subpar alternatives to spiritual gifts and exploration. There's probably a television in your home. How many times have you used it to numb yourself rather than listen to the part of you asking you to switch off and sit in silence?

If you give it some thought, you'll realize that humans have become androids. Why? Almost everyone has a cell phone, that little rectangle that might as well be called Distraction Central. Many are worried about artificial intelligence without realizing it has already been ruling their lives through that little device they carry.

On the surface, it may seem that access to digital information from a wide range of sources is a good thing. However, that can quickly lead to overwhelm. You pick up all kinds of ideas from all kinds of places, and the next thing you know, you're no longer yourself. You become a parrot, repeating other people's perspectives without giving it any thought of your own.

Even if you decide to put your phone away and go for a walk, billboards everywhere vie for your attention. There's so much noise in the world that it's difficult to hear your inner self. This is why meditation is one of the perfect routes to discovering your purpose.

Daily meditation helps you to reduce your stress levels, putting you in a frame of mind where it's easier to pick up on what your higher self is sharing. You shed all the opinions, ideas, and perspectives that aren't yours and are left with nothing but your *Self.*

Meditation is also helpful because it encourages you to self-reflect and improve your self-awareness. If you can't do that, you won't hear the intuitive nudges you receive from the Divine. With all that said, here's a meditation to help you reconnect with your soul's purpose and express your higher self. These instructions will help you discover your highest purpose.

1. Make sure you're not wearing anything uncomfortable or tight.
2. Find somewhere quiet, away from distractions and disturbances. Whether you sit or lie down during your meditation is up to you. Sit or lie down, but choose a position where you will stay awake.
3. Close your eyes and bring your attention to your breath. Breathe slowly and deeply. Inhale for four counts, hold for another four, and then exhale for four. Do you find the counts uncomfortable? In that case, inhale until your belly rises, hold your breath for as long as you can manage, and then exhale. You may notice your exhale is longer than your inhale. That's natural.
4. When you feel centered, picture yourself surrounded by a white light. This light feels warm to your skin. It fills your heart with sacred peace and joy. It is the light of your higher self.
5. Say in your mind or aloud, "Thank you for showing me my soul's purpose." As you repeat this like a mantra, contemplate what you're saying. By offering thanks, you're assuming and accepting that you've already received the answer you seek. So, this is how you learn your purpose – if not in this session, then in the coming days and weeks.
6. As you repeat this mantra, let the light envelope you and let it fill you on the inside as well.
7. Continue to bask in the feeling of gratitude until your meditation session is done. On some days, when you don't have enough time, a timer will be useful. On others, you may continue to bask in this feeling of thankfulness for as long as you like.
8. When you're ready, bring your attention back to your breath. Become more aware of your body. Give your fingers and toes a little wriggle to ground yourself. When you're ready, open your eyes.
9. Get your journal and write about your experience, including ideas and whatever visions or sensations you picked up.

Before moving on to the next method for discovering your soul's purpose, please understand that this is not usually something people discover in a day. That's not to say it's impossible to have that experience after your very first meditation session with this intention, but it's important to keep the right perspective and not pressure yourself with unrealistic expectations. Maintain an attitude of trust - divine nonchalance, if you will.

You've put forth the intention, and one thing about intentions is that they must be fulfilled. Each time the question of what you're supposed to do with your life arises in your mind, greet it with thanks in your heart. See the moments you feel confused about your purpose as the birthing pains of its revelation and choose to feel excited instead. This will quicken the manifestation of your answer.

## Automatic Writing to Access Your Soul's Blueprint

Some call it automatic writing. Others call it psychography. Either way, it's the practice of reaching into yourself to draw out wisdom that is beyond your conscious awareness. It's connecting with your soul and your higher self to learn what is essential to know at this point in your life. Automatic writing is a beautiful way to figure out what you're supposed to be doing with your time on Earth. Whether you think this intelligence is coming from your soul, higher self, subconscious mind, or God, with automatic writing, you are allowing the intelligence of the Divine Source to flow through you.

There are so many reasons to take advantage of automatic writing.

1. It induces a state of calmness, grounding you in the present.
2. You'll experience uncommon clarity.
3. You're receiving guidance from the best sources through this practice.
4. Your third eye, throat, and heart chakras will open up and function even better as you practice.
5. You'll develop a more solid trust in your intuition and gut feelings.
6. You'll make wiser decisions than you used to.
7. Your psychic abilities will also improve.

As you practice automatic writing, you'll find it incredibly revealing. As a bonus, in the process of expressing messages from your higher consciousness, you'll be healed on so many levels. Many of the mental blocks, physical issues, and stagnancy people experience in life stem from refusing to express their inner selves. With automatic writing, you're allowing source energy to flow through you, and this energy automatically heals all wounds and opens all blocks.

**How do you practice automatic writing?** Specifically, how can you use this process to help you determine your soul's purpose? It's a straightforward process. Originally, this practice was done with a pen and paper, but with new technology, there's no reason you can't use a word-processing application. Some people prefer to do it the old way, with a good old-fashioned pen and paper, because something about the process of writing feels organic and helps them allow the messages to flow unhindered. It's up to you to practice and see what you prefer.

If you want to get the most out of automatic writing, you should forget about time. Don't expect that you must express everything you're supposed to learn in a matter of minutes. It's a process that will take as long as it takes. If you pressure yourself by trying to fit it all in a specific time frame, you will make it hard to pick up on what your higher self is telling you. Follow these steps to use automatic writing to discover your soul's grandest purpose.

1. Prepare the materials you'll be taking notes with. If you're taking notes with a digital device, please put it on airplane mode and set it to Do-Not-Disturb so you're not distracted by any notifications.
2. Bring your attention to your intention.
3. Take a few minutes to become centered by meditating. As with meditation, automatic writing requires an environment free from distractions and disturbances. So, if you need to inform other people you live with that you need a few moments alone, do so.
4. Now that you're grounded, pick up your writing materials.
5. From this calm state, write down your intention, which is to discover your highest purpose. If you prefer, you could phrase this as a question.
6. Keep writing your intention or question over and over while maintaining your centered state of mind and a soft focus on what you're doing. Alternatively, you could write the question just once and keep it in your mind. Wait for the messages to come.

7. At some point, you'll feel the urge to write something. Flow with that.
8. Throughout this process, your mind must be relaxed. There's no room for logic here, so don't feel like whatever's coming through onto the pages needs to make sense. Even if all you're getting are scribbles at first, trust that they will lead you to something profound with time.
9. At some point, you'll feel like there's nothing further to give. When this happens, don't be dismayed, and don't attempt to force the process to continue. Instead, offer thanks to your higher self and then review what you've written.

Discovering your purpose through psychography may require more than a few sessions, but it works effectively. Your expectations are everything. Don't interpret a seemingly fruitless session as a sign that this doesn't work. If you do, you might as well give up. Keeping your expectations positive and trusting that you already have your answer is a surefire way to get results. It's only a matter of time.

## Finding Your Purpose Through Shamanic Journeying

There's no reason you can't discover the master plan for your life with shamanic journeying. After all, it's an excellent way to meet your guides and other wise and timeless beings who definitely know more about how life works and why you're here now as the personality you are.

If you choose to practice shamanic journeying to learn your soul's purpose, it's best to go to the Lower World. This world is associated with a deep level of transformation that results from introspection.

One of the main reasons many people aren't living up to their fullest potential or exploring their purpose is because of fear. They know they could be so much more, but they're held back by the implications of what it would mean to embody their full selves. This is why the Lower Realm is the best place to go. There, you can come face to face with your fears, discover what past traumatic events are holding you back, and heal from them.

Just as a seed must be planted in the earth before it shoots into the sky, so must you go into the womb of the Lower World first to find your why. You don't have to do this alone. You'll be accompanied by your guides.

Here's how the process works.

1. You need to find a quiet place free from disturbances and distractions. If it helps, you can set the mood by dimming the lights, using candles, lighting incense, or whatever else will make you feel tuned in to the spiritual realm.
2. Play a shamanic drumming track in the background, or focus on the sound and feeling of your heartbeat.
3. Lie down or sit comfortably. Close your eyes and focus on taking deep, relaxing breaths, releasing tension with every exhale.
4. When you feel grounded in the moment, imagine a bubble of brilliant golden white light that surrounds you, keeping you safe and protected for the journey to come.
5. Bring your mind to your intention. Remember, the goal of this journey is to discover your soul's highest purpose. Firmly and softly state your intention.
6. In your mind's eye, see yourself at the base of the biggest tree you could possibly imagine. Notice the opening at the base of the tree. Walk towards it and enter through the opening.
7. Now you're inside the tree's trunk. Notice the stairs that lead down into the Lower Realm. Mindfully descend, feeling each step beneath your feet. Notice the sense of going deeper and deeper into the core of the universe.
8. As you journey down, you'll notice the world around you is changing. This tells you that you are approaching your destination.
9. You have now arrived. Take a moment to look around you and study what you see. Notice the environment as well as any sentient beings around, human or otherwise, and trust that you are safe and protected.
10. State your intention to meet your guides as you walk further into this realm from its entrance. When they show up, you'll know it because their energy will feel familiar and safe to you.
11. Once you meet your guides, ask them about your soul's purpose. Pay attention to how you feel and the thoughts that arise after asking. You don't always receive communication using words. Sometimes, it will be like a block of thought coming into your mind, and at other times, it will simply be a feeling or energy. Whatever you receive, trust that it is your answer.

12. If the answer seems unclear, don't let that discourage you. Instead, thank your guides for offering you their time and guidance. Ask them to make the meaning of their message clearer to you over the coming days and weeks, and thank them for doing so. You should also thank them for their presence.
13. Return to the entrance of the Lower Realm and make your way back up the stairs. Once you're out of the World Tree, thank it for allowing you access to the Lower Realm.
14. Bring your attention back to your breath. Wiggle your toes and fingers to become more present in your body. When you're ready, open your eyes.
15. Get your journal and record every memory and feeling you received during your journey. Take a few moments to ponder the meaning of the message you got, putting it in the context of discovering your reason for being.

Note that you may not get the full picture of your guide's message to you after a session or two, but it is not something to worry about. Live every day with the intention of discovering and understanding their message more than before. Pay attention to the intuitive nudges and signs that come your way. This is how their answer will unfold and make itself plain to you.

## Using Divination to Find Your Why

You've already learned a little bit about divination and how it works. It's an excellent way to find out why you are here. You could work with tarot readings, which require tarot cards. These cards include the Major and Minor Arcana, and each one has its own meaning.

Runes are another excellent choice, with each one representing a theme, word, and sound. Whether you choose tarot cards or runes, you could either interpret them individually or use groups of cards or runes to offer you context.

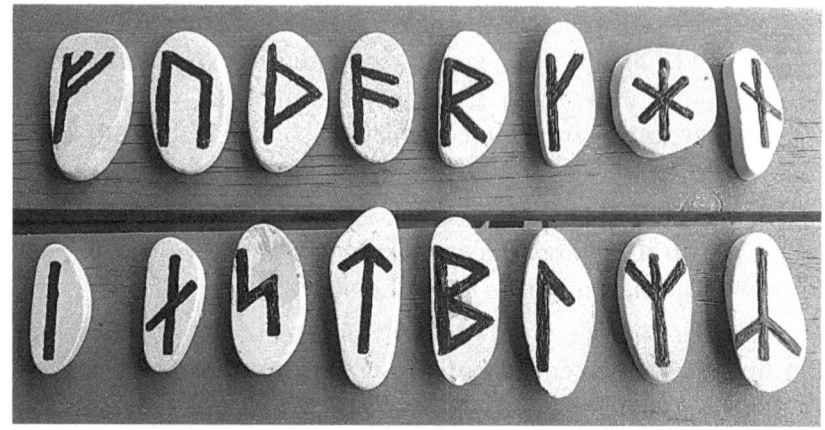

Runes can offer some context.*

One of the easiest and most accessible methods for these practices is pendulum reading. You'll need a pendulum, a weighted object that hangs at the end of a string. You could buy one or create a simple one at home using a piece of thread and a key with a hole. Pass the thread through the hole, then tie it securely with a knot. You now have a makeshift pendulum. No key? No problem. Any other heavy object you can hang from your thread will do. Here's how to use your pendulum:

1. Enter into a meditative state.

2. Take your pendulum in both hands - string and weight included.

3. Breathe golden white light onto the pendulum thrice, imagining that it clears it of all energies that will not serve you. This is how you consecrate it for your use alone and ensure you receive messages from your higher self and other guides who want good things for you.

4. Hold your pendulum in your dominant hand. Let the weight hang freely, swinging as it will.

5. Now, it's time to "calibrate" your pendulum. Ask it a question that could only be answered with a yes, like, "Is my name (your name here)?" Wait and observe the way that it moves.

6. Ask it a question that could only be answered with a no, like "Do I have two heads?" Now, observe the way it moves.

7. Ask two more sets of "yes" and "no" questions so you know what each movement implies.

8. Now that you've connected with your pendulum and know how it swings to say yes and no, set your intention to learn about your soul's purpose.
9. Ask your pendulum if your higher self and spiritual guides are present.
10. If your pendulum swings yes, begin asking simple yes or no questions about your soul's purpose. For instance, you could ask if you are meant to be in the entertainment industry. If it swings "no," keep asking about other industries until it swings "yes."

To make the most of this method, you may want to ask questions about the things you are naturally good at because the odds are they are part of your grand design and soul's plan.

## 5 Tips for Learning Why You're Here

You now have several tools you can use to discover your purpose. Regardless of what you choose, the following tips will help you to succeed.

1. **Pay Attention to the Things That Bring You Joy:** They're clues about what you're meant to be doing. Write about them in your journal when you discover them, and find ways to incorporate these activities into your everyday life and share them with others.
2. **Spend Time Meditating Every Day:** This practice is like sandpaper, polishing off all the unneeded roughness that keeps your purpose from shining brilliantly. It will help you see what matters and what doesn't. The answers you seek are within stillness, silence, and solitude.
3. **Get Creative:** You don't need to be the world's greatest artist, singer, writer, painter, or whatever else. Just find a way to tap into your creative side every day. Everyone has creative abilities within them. Express yourself through art, and you'll find clues about what matters to your soul.
4. Spend Time in a Natural Environment. Nature is a powerful gift. The more time you spend in a natural environment, the easier it will be to pick up on your soul's desires and plans. Your higher self is always speaking to you. Whether you choose to be up in the mountains, by the seashore, or in the heart of the forest, you'll notice nature sharpens your inner ears to hear the guidance you carry within you.

5. **Keep an Open Mind:** If you've always preferred routine, it's time to shake things up. If you always say no to the new and unfamiliar, it's time to ask yourself why. Could it be that your ego knows that's where your true purpose lies? Start saying yes to new opportunities and experiences and see what exciting paths they lead you down.

# Chapter 9: Daily Rituals for Conscious Living

At the start of this book, you learned about consciousness, exploring different perspectives and descriptions. You've learned that consciousness is awareness and that you can be aware of being one thing or another. You also discovered the connection between consciousness and quantum physics, finding the threads that connect these subjects. You also learned about quantum brain mechanics, which explains the origins of consciousness.

You discovered the state of superposition, which is when a particle exists in every possible state it could all at once, only choosing one state in response to an observer and their expectations through the wave function collapse. You understand how entanglement works, but what are the implications? If you're observing something and expecting it to present in a certain way, it does, and then every other thing quantumly entangled with it must mirror that one thing.

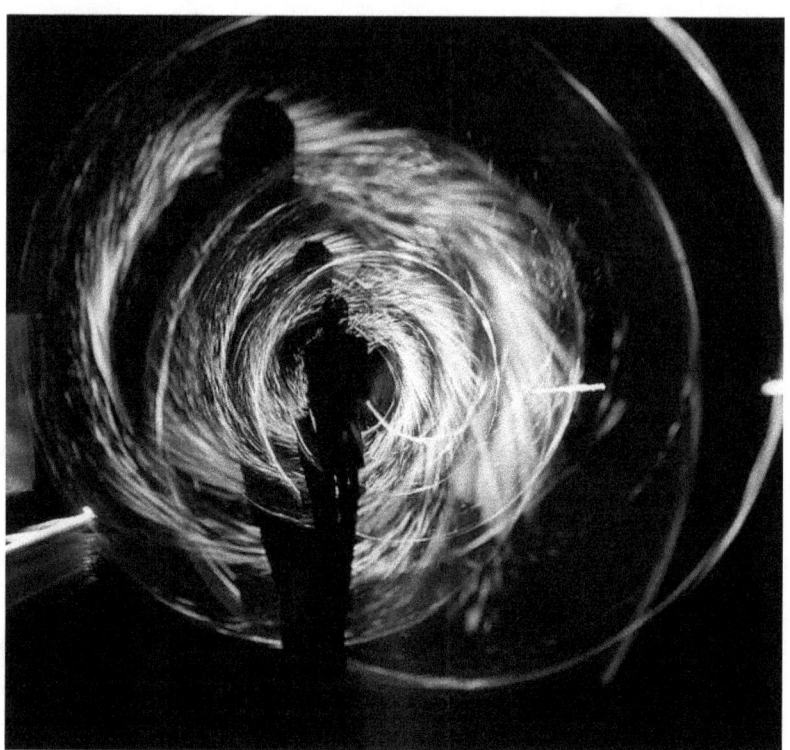

**Tapping into the infinite intelligence of higher consciousness will lead you to live a life that gives you joy and fulfillment.**[50]

To make things plain, every possible version of you and your life exists at the same time. If you've been conscious of being a poor, starving artist, you've used the observer effect to cause a wave collapse function where you live only as a poor, starving artist as opposed to anything else. With entanglement always in action, everything in your life mirrors your identity as an artist who cannot afford to make ends meet.

The implication is that if you want to be a successful artist, you have to "observe" yourself as that. You have to become "conscious" of vision by tapping into higher consciousness, the field of infinite possibility, selecting this preferred state of being, and then causing the wave function collapse that changes your world to reflect your new state of abundance.

You also learned about higher consciousness, and hopefully, you've realized there's no reason to condemn yourself to the struggles of living a life purely from your ego's limited perspective and assumptions of what's possible for you. These practices help you become aware of your higher self, break through limiting paradigms, tap into the infinite intelligence of higher consciousness, and live a life that gives you joy and fulfillment.

To see powerful, permanent change, you need a daily ritual incorporating these powerful quantum physics and consciousness concepts. This chapter will help you with suggestions for practices to make a non-negotiable part of your day. By creating a consistent ritual for your spiritual evolution, there's no limit to the heights you can attain, and you'll turn everything you once considered "impossible" into reality.

## Morning Rituals

Start every day with a ritual and observe how your life changes with time. It's easier to practice your preferred spiritual exercises first thing in the morning before you do anything else because the energy you put out at the start of your day will pave the way for good experiences. At the very least, it will help you handle any negativity better. Suppose you wait until you're in the middle of your day to practice. In that case, you'll have difficulty getting the most out of your ritual – and that's a double guarantee if you've already gone through situations that put you in a bad mood.

If you kick start your day with a spiritual practice, you automatically put yourself in a state of heightened awareness and are more conscious of your choices throughout the day. You're also less susceptible to letting negative emotions get the better of you if some undesirable situation triggers them. You already know about meditation. What else could you do first thing in the morning?

**Set Positive Intentions:** Your intention is how you want something to play out. It's how you'd prefer to experience your day. Even if you're feeling a little doubtful about the power of all this, you could at least set an intention for one thing that you know is within your control, which is your emotional state. By starting your day with the intention to embody a specific emotion or state of being, you give yourself a better chance of feeling how you want to feel.

As you set positive intentions for your emotional state, pay attention to how your day goes. Journaling is an excellent practice that will help you. At the end of each day, reflect on the intention you started with and review how you handled yourself. The more you practice setting positive intentions, the more you'll notice your feelings line up with whatever you intended. This result should give you more than enough evidence of the power of setting positive intentions. From this point on, you can practice setting intentions for specific situations you'd like to experience.

How do you set a positive intention? When you wake up in the morning, immediately begin meditating. Once you feel grounded and your mind is still, turn your attention to your intention. If it helps, you can summarize it in a single word. Then, repeat this word while contemplating what it means to you until you begin to feel it.

Notice where this feeling comes from in your body. Then, move the feeling around your body from head to toe. Imagine it like a white light. After moving this light around, you allow it to permeate your entire body. You can end this session by offering thanks. If you're still battling with the idea of entities other than humans, at least trust that through quantum entanglement, your day should line up with your intention.

You can also set intentions at the end of your day for a good night's rest, dreams, communicating with your guides through visions or dreams, astral travel, etc. You can set intentions whenever you want to. The more you practice and see results, the more likely it is that you'll get used to setting intentions on the fly at different points of your day. You could set them up for productive meetings, interesting interactions, an enjoyable lunch, etc.

**Gratitude:** Gratitude is the cheat code to manifest whatever your heart desires easily and quickly. Many people assume you should only be thankful after receiving something, but did you know you can reverse-engineer the process? Think of it like this. Your desire is a particle. Your thankfulness for having received the desire is another particle. Both particles are quantumly entangled. By choosing to be thankful for receiving your desire, even if you don't have physical evidence of it yet, you are causing a wave function collapse that will lead to the manifestation of the desire.

For people who struggle with all kinds of manifestation techniques, gratitude is a simple shortcut. So, what do you desire? Whether it's for your day to go a particular way or for something more specific and tangible, try gratitude. A simple way to practice this is to first get into your centered state from meditation and then say, "Thank you," while contemplating what it is you're thankful for.

One of the reasons gratitude is so effective is because you're skipping the middle bits of how your desire will come to be and cutting to the aftermath when you've already received it. So, make this a daily practice.

Another way to practice gratitude is by making lists of things for which you are thankful. It doesn't have to be a long list. Even just listing three to five things every day that you appreciate will go a long way to activating the magic of gratitude in your life. How? You'll experience even more to be grateful for. There may be days when you feel like you can't come up with a single thing to appreciate. There's no reason to beat yourself up for that! It's enough to revisit old lists you've made and let your heart be full of thanks for them.

A common mistake people make is assuming that it's about the words. Without actually feeling thankful, you could say "thank you" until the cows come home and not experience any of the lovely gifts gratitude gives you. So, how do you generate the feeling? Recognizing all the reasons why you're thankful is a good thing, and how - despite many people not having those same blessings - you get to experience them!

## Mind-Body Connection Practices

Many people experience anxiety, fear, and worry because they are in their heads and not in their bodies. Mind-body connection practices are designed to move you from that chaotic mental space into just being in the here and now, the same way your body is.

**Yoga:** Yoga will show you in real-time how your mind and body are connected. As you practice it each day, you'll discover that you're not only getting fitter but also more present and grounded. Remember, this state of presence is essential for remaining connected to higher consciousness, which is why you picked up this book in the first place. Visit your local Yoga instructors. Try a class with several of them to find the best fit for you.

Yoga will show you in real-time how your mind and body are connected.[51]

**Tai Chi:** Tai Chi is a moving meditation that heals your body. This Chinese martial art puts you firmly in your body, giving your mind a chance to go to bed. As a result, you'll take the relaxation you feel from each session into other aspects of your life, operating with a calm and clear mind – the kind of mind that's conducive to picking up on messages from the spirit world. The inner peace a consistent Tai Chi practice offers you is beyond compare. Every move is synchronized to the breath, making it impossible to be anything but present. Look out for classes around you to find one where you feel comfortable.

**Breathwork:** Breathwork is another stress-relieving practice that will help you maintain your higher consciousness connection. It's one way to practice mindfulness, requiring you to control your breath in various ways. If you're like most people, you probably take shallow breaths. The problem with breathing this way is that you activate your autonomic nervous system, which means you are constantly stressed out. You keep your body stuck in the fight-flight-freeze-fawn state. These responses are great when you're in danger, but when you're stuck in this state for too long, it's terrible for your health.

**Breathwork:** will help you activate your parasympathetic nervous system, which allows you to rest and feel at ease. What's more, it puts you in a meditative state, keeping you in the present where it's easier to release negative emotions, beliefs, thoughts, and behaviors that keep you from living authentically. Here are a few versions of breathwork practices you can take advantage of right away.

1. **Diaphragmatic Breathing:** Lie flat on your back, with a hand on your chest and the other on your stomach while you breathe. To inhale, go slowly and use your nostrils. You should feel your stomach lifting your hand. To exhale, release the breath slowly through your slightly open mouth so the hand on your belly goes back down. Keep going for as long as you want.

2. **4-4-4-4- Breathing:** While lying flat on your back, inhale through your nostrils for four counts, hold your breath for four counts, exhale through your slightly open mouth for four counts, and hold your breath for four counts. Repeat this process, stopping when you're ready to or when your timer goes off.

# Law of Attraction Visualization Techniques

Visualization involves using your imagination to see the version of the world you'd prefer to be in. When you visualize something, you are using the observer effect to select your reality through the wave function collapse mechanism. You're channeling your formless consciousness (I AM) toward embodying a specific form (that). This is the esoteric interpretation of the Biblical phrase, "I Am that I Am."

Visualization involves using your imagination to see the version of the world you'd prefer to be in.[53]

You can use vision boards to visualize. Clip every picture and article that sums up the essence of what you want to create and put them up where you can see it first thing in the morning and last thing at night.

Another method is the "State Akin to Sleep" technique by Neville Goddard. It's a simple, three-step process:

1. Know what you want.

2. Construct a scene that could only happen after you receive what you want (not before and not during). Make it a concise scene. If you want a promotion, the scene could be your boss shaking your hand and saying, "Congratulations."

3. Lie down and convince yourself that you're sleepy by repeating, "I feel sleepy." Then, from this drowsy state, loop the scene you created over and over, making sure you pay attention to the sights, sounds, and other sensations in that scene.

## Other Rituals

1. Try taking midday awareness breaks. In the middle of your day, you could meditate, visualize, set intentions, or do anything else to help you realign with higher consciousness.

2. Afternoon and evening reflections are great for developing self-awareness. You could talk to your higher self through channeling, using a recording app to play back those conversations later or transcribe them automatically. With this practice, you're reflecting on the events of the day so far and reminding yourself of your intention to remain aware of your interconnection with others, your guides, your higher self, and, of course, higher consciousness.

3. Dreamwork is a great tool to incorporate as a ritual. Begin by writing down whatever you remember of your dreams every night to improve your recall. If you think you don't dream, at least write down how you feel when you wake up. When you begin recalling your dreams, you can set the intention to use this state to do your higher consciousness work every night before bed or whenever you want to take a nap.

With these daily rituals, you'll experience an increase in your consciousness and self-awareness. You go from living a life full of "accidents" to living on purpose and in alignment with your highest ideals. Consistency is the secret to getting results with these rituals, and the more you practice, the more pieces of the puzzle to your ultimate purpose you'll collect and put together.

# Conclusion

You've been given every tool possible to begin the process of living consciously. The fact that you've read up to this point suggests that you will likely experience the spiritual expansion you desire.

There may be days when you don't feel like you're in the mood to practice your rituals. This is a natural part of being human. Remember, connecting to higher consciousness is more of an ebb and flow. There's no reason to beat yourself up for feeling like you've fallen off the wagon. On the days when you find it difficult to follow through, if you can commit at least three to five minutes to one practice, that should still keep you progressing – but that's no excuse to become complacent either.

This book is only a guideline and not a rule book. So, if you feel intuitively led to tweak certain practices or try something new, follow your hunch. Remember, no one can lead you better than your higher self. Trust every intuitive nudge you receive. Learn to do this without question, and you'll be amazed at the magical world that reveals itself to you.

There are so many resources available to help you along your journey. An open mind and avail yourself of everyone you come across. Whether you're reading a book or watching a video, always check in with your gut. How will your soul let you know what messages to keep and what to discard? Follow what is designed for you rather than do everything recommended to you because you're hoping something sticks. Even in this book, certain exercises may have caught your interest more than others. Your interest is a clue from your higher self, telling you that you should explore this.

You're about to begin a journey that will pay dividends. Ask anyone who's found their connection to higher consciousness, and they will tell you they have no idea how they could have lived without it.

If you're struggling with anything, whether it's consistency or focus, don't forget you're not alone. You have guides to assist you toward the fulfillment of your grand design. You could never be too much trouble to them. Ask, and it will be given – every time. Thank yourself for having the courage to begin this adventure. It's nothing to sneeze at, but in the end, you'll be glad you answered the call of the source of all life.

If you enjoyed this book, I'd greatly appreciate a review on Amazon because it helps me to create more books that people want. It would mean a lot to hear from you.

**To leave a review:**
1. Open your camera app.
2. Point your mobile device at the QR code.
3. The review page will appear in your web browser.

*Thanks for your support!*

# Here's another book by Mari Silva that you might like

# Your Free Gift
# (only available for a limited time)

Thanks for getting this book! If you want to learn more about various spirituality topics, then join Mari Silva's community and get a free guided meditation MP3 for awakening your third eye. This guided meditation mp3 is designed to open and strengthen ones third eye so you can experience a higher state of consciousness. Simply visit the link below the image to get started.

https://spiritualityspot.com/meditation

### Or, Scan the QR code!

# References

Banik, M., Gazi, Md. R., Ghosh, S., & Kar, G. (2013). Degree of Complementarity Determines the Nonlocality in Quantum Mechanics. Physical Review A, 87(5). https://doi.org/10.1103/physreva.87.052125

Buhrman, H., Cleve, R., Massar, S., & de Wolf, R. (2010). Nonlocality and Communication Complexity. Reviews of Modern Physics, 82(1), 665-698. https://doi.org/10.1103/revmodphys.82.665

Clegg, B. (2009). The God Effect: Quantum Entanglement, Science's Strangest Phenomenon. St. Martin's Griffin.

Dyson, F. (2013). Is a Graviton Detectable? International Journal of Modern Physics A, 28(25), 1330041. https://doi.org/10.1142/s0217751x1330041x

Filk, T., & Albrecht von Müller. (2009). Quantum Physics and Consciousness: The Quest for a Common Conceptual Foundation. Mind and Matter, 7(1).

Hayes, L. J. (1997). Understanding Mysticism. The Psychological Record, 47(4), 573-596. https://doi.org/10.1007/bf03395247

Hirshfeld, A. C. (2000). BOOK REVIEW: String Theory. Volume I: An Introduction to the Bosonic String. by Joseph Polchinski. String Theory. Volume II: Superstring Theory And Beyond. by Joseph Polchinski. General Relativity and Gravitation, 32(11), 2235-2237. https://doi.org/10.1023/a:1001959811458

Horgan, J. (2004). Rational Mysticism. HMH.

Jackson, G. (2022, September 28). What is the Main Difference between Classical Physics and Quantum Physics? [Fact Checked!]. Physics Network. https://physics-network.org/what-is-the-main-difference-between-classical-physics-and-quantum-physics/

Kenneth William Ford. (2011). 101 Quantum Questions: What You Need To Know About The World You Can't See. Harvard University Press.

MacIsaac, T. (2018). A New Theory of Consciousness: The Mind Exists as a Field Connected to the Brain - Science and Nonduality (SAND). Science and Nonduality (SAND). https://scienceandnonduality.com/article/a-new-theory-of-consciousness-the-mind-exists-as-a-field-connected-to-the-brain/

Mansuripur, M. (2009). Classical Optics and its Applications. In Cambridge University Press (2nd ed.). Cambridge University Press. https://www.cambridge.org/core/books/classical-optics-and-its-applications/7E0D316A0E283CAE3876B7DAC50621B4

Misra, B., & Sudarshan, E. C. G. (1977). The Zeno's Paradox in Quantum Theory. JMP, 18(4), 756-763. https://doi.org/10.1063/1.523304

Nomura, Y., Poirier, B., & Terning, J. (2018). Quantum Physics, Mini Black Holes, and the Multiverse: Debunking Common Misconceptions in Theoretical Physics. Springer International Publishing.

Oppenheim, J., & Wehner, S. (2010). The Uncertainty Principle Determines the Nonlocality of Quantum Mechanics. Science, 330(6007), 1072-1074. https://doi.org/10.1126/science.1192065

Ponte, D., & Schäfer, L. (2013). Carl Gustav Jung, Quantum Physics and the Spiritual Mind: A Mystical Vision of the Twenty-First Century. Behavioral Sciences, 3(4), 601-618. https://doi.org/10.3390/bs3040601

Popescu, S. (2014). Nonlocality Beyond Quantum Mechanics. Nature Physics, 10(4), 264-270. https://doi.org/10.1038/nphys2916

Posner, M. I. (1994). Attention: the Mechanisms of Consciousness. Proceedings of the National Academy of Sciences, 91(16), 7398-7403. https://doi.org/10.1073/pnas.91.16.7398

Pratt, D. (2007). Consciousness, Causality, and Quantum Physics. NeuroQuantology, 1(1). https://doi.org/10.14704/nq.2003.1.1.5

Qian, X.-F., Vamivakas, A., & Eberly, J. (2017). Emerging Connections: Quantum and Classical Optics The blurring of the classical-quantum boundary points to new directions in optics. https://arxiv.org/ftp/arxiv/papers/1712/1712.10040.pdf

Rae, A. I. M. (2013). Quantum physics, Illusion or Reality? Cambridge University Press.

Rogalski, M. S., & Palmer, S. B. (1999). Quantum Physics. Gordon And Breach Science Publishers.

Silverman, M. P. (2008). Quantum Superposition. Springer Science & Business Media.

Simon, C. (2019). Can Quantum Physics Help Solve the Hard Problem of Consciousness? Journal of Consciousness Studies, 26(5, 6).

Stapp, H. P. (1999). Attention, Intention, and Will in Quantum Physics. Journal of Consciousness Studies, 6(8-9).

https://www.ingentaconnect.com/content/imp/jcs/1999/00000006/f0020008/971

Tricycle. (2020). What is Dependent Origination? Buddhism for Beginners. https://tricycle.org/beginners/buddhism/dependent-origination/

Zeilinger, A. (1999). Experiment and the Foundations of Quantum Physics. Reviews of Modern Physics, 71(2), S288–S297. https://doi.org/10.1103/revmodphys.71.s288

Acacio, J., Montemayor, C., & Springerlink (Online Service. (2019). Quanta and Mind: Essays on the Connection between Quantum Mechanics and Consciousness. Springer International Publishing.

Bertoldi, C. (2012). Inside the Other Side: Soul Contracts, Life Lessons, and How Dead People Help Us, Between Here and Heaven. Harper Collins.

Byrne, L. (2011). Angels in My Hair: A Memoir. Three Rivers Press.

Cannon, D. (1993). Between Death & Life: Conversations with a Spirit. Ozark Mountain Publishing.

Cannon, D. (2009). Five Lives Remembered. Ozark Mountain Publishing.

Carrington, H., & Muldoon, S. J. (1981). The Phenomena of Astral Projection. Sun Publishing (NM).

Crabbé, R. (2019). The Three Shamanic Worlds. RoelCrabbe.com. https://www.roelcrabbe.com/the-three-shamanic-worlds/

Delamothe, M. (2023). Shamanic Journeying and Astral Projection: What's the Difference? SignsMystery. https://signsmystery.com/shamanic-astral-difference/

Gergar, L. (2010). What is the Higher Self? Channel Higher Self. https://channelhigherself.com/blog/what-is-the-higher-self-2/

Gizzi, C. (2016). What Is Higher Consciousness and How Can We Access It? Fearless Soul - Inspirational Music & Life-Changing Thoughts. https://iamfearlesssoul.com/what-is-higher-consciousness-and-how-can-we-access-it/

Greene, B. (2012). The Hidden Reality: Parallel Universes and the Deep Laws of the Cosmos. Penguin, Impr., Cop.

Gribbin, J. R. (2009). In Search of the Multiverse: Parallel Worlds, Hidden Dimensions, and the Ultimate Quest for the Frontiers of Reality. Wiley.

Ingerman, S. (2020). Shamanic Journeying: A Beginner's Guide. Sounds True.

Itzhak Bentov. (2000). A Brief Tour of Higher Consciousness: A Cosmic Book on the Mechanics of Creation. Inner Traditions.

Luna, A. (2017). Automatic Writing: How to Channel Your Soul's Wisdom. LonerWolf. https://lonerwolf.com/automatic-writing/

Luna, A. (2021). Soul Purpose: 5 Gateways to Finding Your Destiny. LonerWolf. https://lonerwolf.com/soul-purpose/

Psychic Radar. (2023). Exploring Past Life Regression: Unveiling the Secrets of Previous Lifetimes. Psychic Radar. https://psychicradar.com/articles/exploring-past-life-regression/

Roberts, J. (1994). Seth Speaks: The Eternal Validity of the Soul. Amber-Allen Publ., New World Library.

Rochelle, K. (2023). Understanding Spirit Guides. Positively Kimberly. https://www.positivelykimberly.com/understanding-spirit-guides/#How_to_Connect_with_Your_Spirit_Guides

Scalisi, A. (2022, July 15). Complete List of 22 Abraham Hicks Processes + How To Use Them. The Haven Shoppe. https://thehavenshoppe.com/22-abraham-hicks-processes/

Sharma, S. (2023). Breathwork 101: 5 Simple Breathwork Techniques for Beginners. Calm Sage – Your Guide to Mental and Emotional Well-Being. https://www.calmsage.com/breathwork-techniques/

Thomas, J. J. (2022). Higher Consciousness Demystified. Heart Speak. https://medium.com/heart-speak/higher-consciousness-demystified-80042c9fc9be#bypass

Tolle, E. (2016). A New Earth: Awakening to Your Life's Purpose. London, UK Penguin Books.

Tolle, E. (2018). The Power of Now: A Guide to Spiritual Enlightenment. Hachette Australia

# Image Sources

[1] Designed by Freepik. https://img.freepik.com/free-photo/atom-science-biotechnology-blue-neon-graphic_53876-167297.jpg?t=st=1712095432~exp=1712099032~hmac=56d0a39abad98fe0489.5eb12e59f753030c1892186665aa0b00ec0a86a17b798&w=1060

[2] https://picryl.com/media/max-planck-1933-1bf0ff

[3] https://picryl.com/media/richard-feynman-1988-2d6dca

[4] https://www.flickr.com/photos/7725050@N06/631503428

[5] Designed by Freepik. https://www.freepik.com/free-photo/chemical-element-arrangement-still-life_16691170.htm#fromView=search&page=2&position=16&uuid=cbd7f1b0-2c6a-4ea7-84db-dbb5908fa2d9

[6] https://pixel17.com, CC BY-SA 2.0 <https://creativecommons.org/licenses/by-sa/2.0>, via Wikimedia Commons https://upload.wikimedia.org/wikipedia/commons/9/9a/Niels_Bohr_Portrait.jpg

[7] https://pixabay.com/photos/prism-light-spectrum-optics-6174502/

[8] https://www.needpix.com/photo/download/84526/einstein-formula-mathematics-equation-equations-formulas-free-pictures-free-photos-free-images

[9] Argonne National Laboratory, , ATTRIBUTION-NONCOMMERCIAL-SHAREALIKE 2.0 GENERIC, CC BY-NC-SA 2.0 <https://creativecommons.org/licenses/by-nc-sa/2.0/>https://www.flickr.com/photos/argonne/5039459604

[10] https://picryl.com/media/arthur-compton-1927-91b473

[11] astroshots42Follow, ATTRIBUTION 2.0 GENERIC, CC BY 2.0 <https://creativecommons.org/licenses/by/2.0/>https://www.flickr.com/photos/astro-pics/8468331718

[12] *Original: NekoJaNekoJa  Vector: Johannes Kalliauer, CC BY-SA 4.0 <https://creativecommons.org/licenses/by-sa/4.0>, via Wikimedia Commons. https://commons.wikimedia.org/wiki/File:Double-slit.svg*

[13] *ATTRIBUTION-SHAREALIKE 3.0 UNPORTED, CC BY-SA 3.0 <https://creativecommons.org/licenses/by-sa/3.0/deed.en>https://upload.wikimedia.org/wikipedia/commons/7/77/Photoelectric_effect.png*

[14] *Theresa Knott from en.wikipedia, CC BY-SA 3.0 <http://creativecommons.org/licenses/by-sa/3.0/>, via Wikimedia Commons https://commons.wikimedia.org/wiki/File:Stern-Gerlach_experiment.PNG*

[15] *Master of the Universe 322, CC BY-SA 4.0 <https://creativecommons.org/licenses/by-sa/4.0>, via Wikimedia Commons https://upload.wikimedia.org/wikipedia/commons/7/75/Physics-3864568_960_720.png*

[16] *https://www.pexels.com/photo/an-artist-s-illustration-of-artificial-intelligence-ai-this-image-represents-how-machine-learning-is-inspired-by-neuroscience-and-the-human-brain-it-was-created-by-novoto-studio-as-par-17483868/*

[17] *TEDxSydney, ATTRIBUTION-NONCOMMERCIAL-NODERIVS 2.0 GENERIC, CC BY-NC-ND 2.0 < https://creativecommons.org/licenses/by-nc-nd/2.0/> https://www.flickr.com/photos/tedxsydney/5779378540*

[18] *Yancho Sabev, CC BY-SA 3.0 <https://creativecommons.org/licenses/by-sa/3.0>, via Wikimedia Commons https://upload.wikimedia.org/wikipedia/commons/2/2a/The_14th_Dalai_Lama_FEP.jpg*

[19] *https://www.pexels.com/photo/woman-lying-down-on-floor-relaxing-and-meditating-6998214/*

[20] *Designed by Freepik. https://img.freepik.com/free-photo/mystical-numerology-scene_52683-107763.jpg?t=st=1712100292~exp=1712103892~hmac=cb45e539f861710558dd2229477b9caf37f47e6752aa6296bd82769a8bf50c66&w=740*

[21] *Pablo Carlos Budassi, CC BY-SA 4.0 <https://creativecommons.org/licenses/by-sa/4.0>, via Wikimedia Commons https://upload.wikimedia.org/wikipedia/commons/3/32/Earth_and_Universe.jpg*

[22] *https://www.needpix.com/photo/download/1733437/lego-background-lego-building-blocks-pattern-lego-bricks-shape-design-education-toy-pattern*

[23] *https://www.publicdomainpictures.net/en/view-image.php?image=527494&picture=quantum-physics-waves-and-particles*

[24] *https://picryl.com/media/eth-bib-jung-carl-gustav-1875-1961-portrait-portr-14163-cropped-c7875d*

[25] *Designed by Freepik. https://www.freepik.com/free-photo/network-concept-with-colorful-thread_15292480.htm#fromView=search&page=1&position=1&uuid=9da01092-4a93-48ce-9ba7-196234a14a3e*

[26] *alfonso.saborido, ATTRIBUTION 2.0 GENERIC, CC BY 2.0 <https://creativecommons.org/licenses/by/2.0/> https://www.flickr.com/photos/28063292@N02/22560032539*

[27] *Peter Morgan, ATTRIBUTION-NONCOMMERCIAL-NODERIVS 2.0 GENERIC, <https://creativecommons.org/licenses/by-nc-nd/2.0/>*

https://www.flickr.com/photos/pmorgan/3189477502

[28] https://pixabay.com/photos/parallel-world-parallel-universe-3488497/

[29] Designed by freepik. https://www.freepik.com/free-vector/gradient-surrealist-galaxy-illustration_45183512.htm

[30] Designed by freepik. https://www.freepik.com/free-photo/brown-eye-bright-background_31499094.htm

[31] https://www.pexels.com/photo/woman-in-pink-sports-bra-and-black-leggings-doing-yoga-on-yoga-mat-3823076/

[32] Designed by freepik. https://www.freepik.com/free-photo/ultra-detailed-nebula-abstract-wallpaper-5_39994515.htm

[33] Designed by freepik.: https://www.freepik.com/free-vector/hand-drawn-mindfulness-concept-with-characters_16692663.htm

[34] Designed by freepik. Source: https://www.freepik.com/free-photo/medium-shot-human-silhouette-nature_38689099.htm

[35] Designed by freepik. https://www.freepik.com/free-photo/full-shot-super-woman-with-superpowers_38170134.htm

[36] Designed by freepik. https://www.freepik.com/free-photo/3d-render-brain-with-glitter-explosion-effect_987581.htm

[37] Designed by freepik. https://www.freepik.com/free-photo/fantasy-astral-wallpaper-composition_39425682.htm

[38] Designed by freepik. https://www.freepik.com/free-photo/glowing-satellite-orbits-planet-star-filled-galaxy-generated-by-ai_40968223.htm

[39] Designed by freepik. https://www.freepik.com/free-vector/gradient-surrealist-galaxy-illustration_45199603.htm

[40] Designed by freepik. https://www.freepik.com/free-vector/gradient-surrealist-galaxy-illustration_45183518.htm

[41] https://www.freepik.com/free-photo/numerology-concept-composition_38110409.htm

[42] Designed by freepik. https://www.pexels.com/photo/white-and-black-wolf-397857/

[43] Designed by freepik. https://www.pexels.com/photo/stone-sculpture-of-an-angel-with-a-book-against-clouded-sky-8592167/

[44] Designed by freepik. https://www.freepik.com/free-photo/high-angle-woman-reading-tarot-home_39886546.htm

[45] https://pixabay.com/photos/time-clock-time-spiral-spiral-3103599/

[46] https://pixabay.com/photos/body-ghost-soul-religion-woman-2976731/

[47] https://pixabay.com/photos/bible-holy-spirit-jesus-hope-2989432/

[48] https://pixabay.com/photos/sky-love-spiritual-above-top-3983433/

[49] Runologe, CC BY-SA 4.0 <https://creativecommons.org/licenses/by-sa/4.0>, via Wikimedia Commons.
https://commons.wikimedia.org/wiki/File:02_Runes_of_the_Younger_Futhark_painted_on_little_s

tones_-_Runen_des_j%C3%BCngeren_Futhark_auf_kleine_Steine_gemalt.jpg

[50] https://www.pexels.com/photo/silhouette-of-person-holding-sparkler-digital-wallpacpr-266429/

[51] https://www.pexels.com/photo/woman-practicing-yoga-3822906/

[52] *designed by freepik.* https://www.freepik.com/free-photo/collage-numerology-concept_35858713.htm#

www.ingramcontent.com/pod-product-compliance
Lightning Source LLC
Chambersburg PA
CBHW072156200426
43209CB00052B/1270